Horváth: a study

Horváth: a study

by

IAN HUISH

Modern Languages Department
Westminster School

HEINEMANN

LONDON

ROWMAN AND LITTLEFIELD

TOTOWA, NEW JERSEY

Heinemann Educational Books Ltd
22 Bedford Square, London WC1B 3HH

LONDON EDINBURGH MELBOURNE AUCKLAND
HONG KONG SINGAPORE KUALA LUMPUR NEW DELHI
IBADAN NAIROBI JOHANNESBURG
KINGSTON PORT OF SPAIN

First published 1980 by Heinemann Educational Books
First published in the United States 1980
by Rowman and Littlefield, Totowa, N.J.

British Library CIP Data

Huish, Ian
  Horváth.—(Students' guides to European literature).
  1. Horváth, Ödön von—Criticism and interpretation
  I. Series
  832′.9′12   PT2617.0865Z/

  ISBN 0–435–38400–7

  ISBN (US) . 0–8476–6269–1

Set, printed and bound in Great Britain by
Fakenham Press Limited, Fakenham, Norfolk

Contents

in memory of Max Brandt

Foreword

Most of the guides in this series have been concerned with writers whose work is already well known in this country. In the case of Ödön von Horváth it has been necessary to write a guide that will inevitably serve as an introduction to many readers. While I have quoted extensively from Horváth's work and attempted to give the flavour of his language as much as possible, my approach has been deliberately selective: I have chosen the 'Volksstücke' and the last novels as my main areas of study, referring to other works where this seemed useful and devoting a chapter to a selection of his later plays.

All the translations are my own, except for those from *Geschichten aus dem Wiener Wald*. Here I have used the published text of *Tales from the Vienna Woods* translated by Christopher Hampton, with only minor adaptations. The performance of this play at the National Theatre in 1977 marked an historic event: it was the first stage production in England of a Horváth play. Its success led to the smaller scale but no less impressive production of *Don Juan comes back from the War*, also at the National Theatre and translated by Christopher Hampton. I am particularly indebted to him for the interest that he has shown in this book and for his help.

I would also like to thank Brian Masters and Professor Walter Huder, director of the Horváth Archives in Berlin, for their help and encouragement over the past two years. My thanks too are due to Stephen Baister for reading the manuscript and making many helpful suggestions; to Dr Hugh Rank for kindly letting me read the introduction and notes to his edition of *Geschichten aus dem Wiener Wald*; to Suzie Scragg who so patiently typed the manuscript, and most of all to my wife for her support and help throughout.

The page references are all taken from the Suhrkamp Werk-ausgabe of Horváth's collected works and are referred to as *G.W.* Only in the chapter on the novels have I added the pagination of the Harrap edition of *Jugend ohne Gott*. I am grateful to Suhrkamp Verlag and to Thomas Sessler Verlag for their kind permission to quote extensively from Horváth's works, both in the original and in translations.

IAN HUISH

1

Biographical Introduction

Geboren bin ich am 9. Dezember 1901, und zwar in Fiume an der Adria, nachmittags um dreiviertelfünf (nach einer anderen Überlieferung um halb fünf). Als ich zweiunddreißig Pfund wog, verließ ich Fiume, trieb mich teils in Venedig und teils auf dem Balkan herum und erlebte allerhand, u.a. die Ermordung S.M. des Königs Alexanders von Serbien samt seiner Ehehälfte. Als ich 1,20 Meter wurde, zog ich nach Budapest und lebte dort bis 1,21 Meter. War dortselbst ein eifriger Besucher zahlreicher Kinderspielplätze und fiel durch mein verträumtes und boshaftes Wesen unliebenswert auf. Bei einer ungefähren Höhe von 1,52 erwachte in mir der Eros, aber vorerst ohne mir irgendwelche besonderen Schererein zu bereiten—(meine Liebe zur Politik war damals bereits ziemlich vorhanden). Mein Interesse für Kunst, insbesondere für die schöne Literatur, regte sich relativ spät (bei einer Höhe von rund 1,70), aber erst ab 1,79 war es ein Drang, zwar kein unwiderstehlicher, jedoch immerhin. Als der Weltkrieg ausbrach, war ich bereits 1,67 und als er dann aufhörte bereits 1,80 (ich schoß im Krieg sehr rasch empor). Mit 1,69 hatte ich mein erstes ausgesprochen sexuelles Erlebnis—und heute, wo ich längst aufgehört habe zu wachsen (1,84), denke ich mit einer sanften Wehmut an jene ahnungsschwangeren Tage zurück.

Heut geh ich ja nurmehr in die Breite—aber hierüber kann ich Ihnen noch nichts mitteilen, denn ich bin mir halt noch zu nah. (*G.W. 5*, p. 7)

I was born on 9th December`1901, and it was in Fiume on the Adriatic, at 4.45 in the afternoon (4.30 according to another report). When I weighed twenty-two pounds I left Fiume and loafed about partly in Venice and partly in the Balkans, and experienced all sorts of things, among others the murder of H.M. King Alexander of Serbia along with his better half. When I was four foot tall I moved to Budapest and lived there for half an inch. There I was a keen visitor to numerous children's playgrounds and was conspicuous in a rather disagreeable way because of my dreamy and mischievous personality. At a height of about 5'0½" Eros awoke in me, but initially without causing me any bother—(my love of politics was already quite apparent at that time). My interest in art, especially in the classics of literature, stirred relatively late (at a height of about 5'7½") but it only became an urge from 5'11½", not, it is true an irresistible one, but there all the same. When the first World War broke out I was already 5'6", and when it ended I was 6' (I shot up very quickly during the war). At 5'7" I had my first proper sexual experience—and today, now that I have long since stopped growing (6'1"), I think back with tender nostalgia to those portentous days.

Now I only grow outwards it is true—but I can't tell you any more about that, because I'm still too close to myself.

These few laconic lines of autobiography are appropriate in several ways as an introduction to Horváth's life and work. They are reluctant (delivered 'auf Bestellung'—on demand—), as were most of the comments on his own life; they are original and witty, avoiding the almost inevitable banalities of a curriculum vitae; also they show the turbulent atmosphere and rootlessness that were characteristic both of his childhood and of his adult life. His origins were by no means pure German: born of a Hungarian civil servant father and a German–Czech mother in Fiume (now Rijeka), educated in a variety of countries and languages, Horváth rightly described himself as

> eine typisch alt-österreichisch-ungarische Mischung: magyarisch, kroatisch, deutsch, tschechisch—mein Name ist magyarisch, meine Muttersprache ist deutsch. (*G.W. 5*, p. 9)

a typical old Austrian–Hungarian mixture: Magyar, Croatian, German, Czech—my name is Magyar, my mother tongue is German.

Ödön von Horváth was scarcely six months old when the family moved to Belgrade and it was here that his brother Lajos (1903–68) was born. A tutor provided the first teaching at home in Budapest and when his father was posted to Munich in 1909 Ödön remained as a boarder in the Rákóczianum (the Episcopal School) in Budapest, until he followed the family to Munich in 1913 and continued his schooling, first at the Wilhelmsgymnasium and later at the Realschule. Even in these early days he had differences of opinion with his religious education teacher, Dr Heinziger, and throughout his schooldays proved to be an argumentative pupil, unwilling to follow orthodox views unquestioningly. It was at this time too that he first began to develop a true mother tongue:

Erst mit vierzehn Jahren schrieb ich den ersten deutschen Satz. (*G.W. 5*, p. 8)

Only at fourteen did I write my first German sentence.

In Pressburg, where Horváth was sent to school in 1916, he was failed in literature and penned a polemical piece entitled 'Professoren in der Unterwelt' ('Teachers in the Underworld') which nearly earned him expulsion. Once more in Budapest Horváth found himself in a group of young political enthusiasts who took as their figurehead the poet Endre Ady whose radical democratic demands had aroused interest in his writings. Another enthusiasm apparent at this time was for the history of Hungary, and this was later reflected in the play fragment *Dosá*—the only overtly historical drama that Horváth ever wrote.

It was in Vienna, living with his uncle, that Horváth passed his Matura (matriculation) at the Realgymnasium, subsequently returning to Munich where he enrolled at the University to study drama, philosophy and German literature. Although he was a lively participant in Artur Kutscher's drama seminars it appears that Horváth's studies ranged into many other areas as well as those mentioned during his years at University. As with so many episodes in his later life his first 'literary success' came about in an ironic way:

> Durch einen Zufall lernte ich hier in München eines Abends den Komponisten Siegfried Kallenberg kennen. 1920. Kallenberg wandte sich an jenem Abend plötzlich an mich mit der Frage, ob ich ihm nicht eine Pantomime schreiben wolle.—Ich war natürlich ziemlich verdutzt, weil ich es mir gar nicht vorstellen konnte, wieso er mit diesem Anliegen an mich herantritt—ich war doch gar kein Schriftsteller und hatte noch nie in meinem Leben etwas geschrieben. Er muß mich wohl verwechselt haben, dachte ich mir—und ursprünglich wollte ich ihn auch aufklären, dann aber überlegte ich es mir doch anders: warum sollte ich es nicht einmal probieren, eine Pantomime zu schreiben. (*G.W.* 1, p. 10)

> By chance I met the composer Siegfried Kallenberg one evening here in Munich. 1920. Kallenberg suddenly addressed himself to me with the question—wouldn't I like to write a pantomime for him.—I was naturally somewhat bewildered since I could not imagine why he should approach *me* with this request—I was not an author at all and had never in my life written anything. He must have confused me with someone else, I thought—and at first I wanted to correct him, but then I considered it differently: why should I not have a go at writing a pantomime.

Horváth wrote the work, *Das Buch der Tänze* (*The Book of Dances*), and it was duly performed, but he later bought up most of the five hundred copies and destroyed them. He was also at this time writing short stories for the satirical magazine *Simplizissimus* to which Frank Wedekind had been a contributor.

After a time at his parents' house in Murnau and a brief visit to Paris, Horváth made Berlin his base, as did so many other writers of the period. Not only was Berlin the political capital but also the cultural and artistic centre of Germany throughout the twenties and thirties. Horváth wrote of it:

Berlin, die die Jugend liebt, und auch etwas für die Jugend tut, im Gegensatz zu den meisten anderen Städten, die nur die platonische Liebe kennen.
Ich liebe Berlin. (*G.W. 8*, p. 658)

Berlin which loves youth and also does something for the young, in contrast to most other towns which only know Platonic love.
I love Berlin.

It is no coincidence that Horváth writes here of love. He was a man who fascinated women and who was fascinated by them, as his numerous love affairs testify. Physically he was a large, broad-shouldered man, always dressed with a casual elegance. His face was roundish, not particularly handsome, but the eyes had a penetrating gaze that never failed to captivate. All those who knew him speak of his unfailing charm and gentleness of manner. The cafés of Berlin, and even more those of Vienna, were for him more than a place of recreation. Often he would go as early as six o'clock in the morning and sit down to write at one of the marble-topped tables, remaining there all day. In company he was always the centre of interest: the affection for Jewish ghetto humour and mastery of Yiddish that he displayed in conversation are all the more remarkable for their rare appearances in his plays. He also enjoyed the company of 'Liliputaner' (midgets) and was a regular visitor at a 'midget café' near the Prater in Vienna, once commenting that he could not imagine such a thing as a Nazi midget. His attraction to fairgrounds, very much apparent in works such as *Kasimir und Karoline* and *Ein Kind unsever Zeit* (*A Child of our Time*), provided him with another kind of world where human beings were 'on show'. He was a brilliant raconteur and a fine mimic with an ear for dialects as well as for jokes. When presenting his play *Die Bergbahn* to a Berlin theatre he made himself out to be a Bavarian worker who had been involved in the building of the cable railway, and to his amusement was believed by the delighted radicals! There are countless other anecdotes that illustrate his love of acting and his sharp sense of humour. Of the characters in his plays he spoke as of living people with whom he spent most of his time and whose malice, stupidity and bestiality fascinated him. Berlin, its people, its crises, and its decadence, were the material that he needed for his life and work.

The political polarization that was taking place as Germany lumbered from one economic crisis to the next is often reflected in Horváth's writing, and yet it is never the central point; nor did Horváth attempt, as Brecht did, to postulate a political solution to the problems. He remained throughout an observer and an illustrator whose standpoint was formulated in the simplest of terms:

> Wie in allen meinen Stücken versuchte ich auch diesmal, möglichst rücksichtslos gegen Dummheit und Lüge zu sein. (Preface to *Glaube Liebe Hoffnung, G.W. 1*, p. 328)

> As in all my plays I have again attempted in this one to be as ruthless as possible against stupidity and lies.

During the early years in Berlin Horváth worked for the German League of Human Rights and some of the political material available to him provided sources for his writing of the period. Horváth's lifelong friendship with Carl Zuckmayer dates from 1929 and it was Zuckmayer, himself holder of the award, who nominated him for the Kleistpreis in 1931 for his play *Geschichten aus dem Wiener Wald* (*Tales from the Vienna Woods*). Even before this public recognition Horváth had received in 1929 a contract from the publishing house of Ullstein which gave him the freedom to write in whatever form he chose. It is interesting to note that it was after this that he first wrote a novel, *Der ewige Spießer* (*The Eternal Petit Bourgeois*), since this form of writing was later to become his only means of expression. The three years that followed were to be the most successful of Horváth's career: *Italienische Nacht* (*Italian Night*), *Geschichten aus dem Wiener Wald* (*Tales from the Vienna Woods*), *Kasimir und Karoline* and *Glaube Liebe Hoffnung* (*Faith Charity Hope*) all date from the years 1930–3.

Important figures in the theatrical and literary world such as Max Reinhardt, Heinz Hilpert and Franz Theodor Csokor were all among Horváth's circle of friends, as were innumerable actors and actresses from the Berlin theatres. It is therefore all the more surprising that there are no references in either Brecht's or Horváth's writings to any communication between them. It can only remain speculation as to whether the two writers ever met. This was the period when Horváth was at his most active in the literary field and also most engaged in politics. Although he never associated himself with any one political party it is clear that Horváth's sympathies were always with the exploited and defenceless, and his attacks were against the mindless use of politics. Of his *Italienische Nacht* he wrote:

> Es geht nicht gegen die Politik, aber gegen die Masse der Politisierenden, gegen die vor allem in Deutschland sichtbare Versumpfung, den Gebrauch politischer Schlagworte. (*Wiener Allgemeine Zeitung*, 5 July 1931, quoted in *Materialien zu Ödön von Horváth*, p. 186)

> It is not against politics but against the mass of those who dabble in politics, against the dissolution which is above all visible in Germany, the use of political slogans.

1931 saw the first performance of *Italienische Nacht* (*Italian Night*) which the Nazis immediately took as an attack on themselves. In that year Horváth had been called as a witness in the trial following a 'Saalschlacht' in Murnau—he had been present when a group of Nazis came in and violently broke up a Socialist political meeting, such as the one shown in *Italienische Nacht*. His outspoken comments, or rather his honesty, when giving his testimony, assured him the undying hatred of the Nazis. The fact that Horváth received the Kleistpreis—and received it at the instigation of Zuckmayer—incensed the extreme right even further. In the Nazi newspaper, the *Völkischer Beobachter*, Rainer Schlösser wrote a savage attack on Zuckmayer (the 'half-Jew') awarding the prize to Horváth (the 'young Hungarian'). It was this same

Rainer Schlösser who, in February 1933, wrote the damning and grimly prophetic lines:

> Ödön von Horváth besaß die Frechheit, die National-sozialisten anzupöbeln. Seine *Italienische Nacht* zeichnet uns als Feiglinge die durch ein einziges Schimpfwort seitens einer Frau in die Flucht geschlagen werden kön-nen. Wird sich der Ödön noch wundern! (*Völkischer Beobachter* 14 February 1933, quoted in *Materialien zu Ödön von Horváth*, p. 67)

> Ödön von Horváth had the impudence to vilify the National Socialists. His *Italian Night* portrays us as cowards who can be put to flight by one single word of abuse from a woman. Ödön has a surprise coming to him!

It was not long before the prophecy began to come true: after Hitler came to power the Horváth house in Murnau was searched and, following their brief but impressive period of success, Horváth's plays were banned from the German stage. Although his Hungarian passport and his father's position as a diplomat ensured him a certain immunity for the time being, Horváth exiled himself voluntarily, travelling first to Salzburg and then to Vienna. Later in 1933 he married the German singer Maria Elsner in Vienna. She was Jewish, and the marriage, which was dissolved in the following year, was solely designed to help her to escape from Germany by taking on Horváth's nationality.

Despite his first flight from Germany, Horváth returned to Berlin in 1934. It was perhaps less for his avowed aim—to study the Nazis at close quarters—than for a deeper reason: he was drawn to and needed Berlin. He began to work there in the film industry and wrote to friends enthusiastically of the scripts he was writing and of the possibility of a film on the life of the English actor Edmund Kean. After a few months of relative calm the Nazis once again began to harass Horváth and he used the occasion of a trip to Zurich for the première of his play *Hin und her* (*To and fro*) to leave Germany once again. He left in the company of the beautiful actress Wera

Liessem who was to be an almost constant companion in the next few years. He made one final journey back to see his parents in the summer of 1936 but on this occasion was ordered to leave Germany within twenty-four hours.

Although his plays were still being performed (in Vienna, Zurich and Prague for example) Horváth had lost his main German-speaking audience, and his plays of the period no longer focus on the German Kleinbürgertum (petty bourgeoisie). The mood of them is altogether more gloomy, more introspective, and the themes (see chapter 6) increasingly personal ones. By 1937 he had distanced himself from his earlier work and spoke of writing a Human Comedy, fully recognizing that

> das menschliche Leben immer ein Trauerspiel, nur im einzelnen eine Komödie ist. (Quoted in *Materialen zu Ödön von Horváth*, p. 192)
>
> Human life is always a tragedy and only in individual episodes is it a comedy.

Whether because he was denied access to the German theatres or because he felt inspired to use a new form, Horváth began with tremendous enthusiasm to write novels. At the time he was living near Salzburg in the village of Henndorf where Carl Zuckmayer and his wife had a house. The immediate success of *Jugend ohne Gott* (*Youth without God*) which was translated into Danish, English, French, Polish, Swedish, Serbo-Croat and Czech within a year of publication, added further momentum to Horváth's passion for the novel form. He wrote of *Jugend ohne Gott*:

> Ich hab das Buch jetzt nochmals so für mich gelesen, und ich kann mir nicht helfen: mir gfallts auch!—Es ist mir dabei noch etwas aufgefallen, nämlich: daß ich, ohne Absicht, auch zum erstenmal den sozusagen faschistischen Menschen (in Person des Lehrers) geschildert habe, an dem die Zweifel nagen—oder besser gesagt: den Menschen im faschistischen Staate. (Letter to Csokor, quoted in *Materialien zu Ödön von Horváth*, p. 193)

> I've read the book again and I can't help it: I think it's
> good too!—something else occurred to me on reading it and
> that is: that, for the first time and unintentionally, I have
> described the so-called Fascist human being who is gnawed by
> doubts—or, to put that better: the human being in the Fascist
> state.

The letters that he wrote in these days are filled with forebodings: they show a sense of impending doom and, with hindsight, it is all too easy to read into them and into his fear of trees and of the street some preternatural anticipation of his own bizarre death. Certainly this is how many of his friends interpreted their last conversations with him, and this is understandable in the climate which surrounded them all. Two days after Hitler invaded Austria, Horváth left Vienna (on 14 March 1938) and, superstitious of flying, travelled by train from Prague via Budapest, Trieste, Venice and Milan to Zurich. The goal at this time was Amsterdam (where the émigré publisher Allert de Lange had published *Jugend ohne Gott*) and Horváth finally arrived there in the third week of May. It was here that Horváth, who had always been a highly superstitious man, visited a clairvoyant. When he told her of his plan to travel on to Paris (where he had arranged meetings with his French translator, Armand Pierhal, and with the film director, Robert Siodmak) it is reported that she fell into a trance-like state and told him that in Paris there awaited him at the end of May the greatest adventure of his life. According to various friends Horváth arrived in Paris in a state of nervous agitation, avoided using lifts or the métro and remained in his room on the last day of May. On June 1st, Horváth's mood seemed to be one of relief: in the afternoon he went to the cinema with friends to see *Snow White and the Seven Dwarfs*. When he left them early in the evening a violent summer storm blew up and Horváth took shelter under a tree with a group of passers-by. A gust of wind broke off a rotten branch which fell, hitting him on the back of the head and killing him instantly. No one else was injured.

One of the items found in the dead man's pocket was a cigarette packet with a poem written on it:

> Und die Leute werden sagen
> In fernen blauen Tagen
> Wird es einmal recht
> Was falsch ist und was echt
>
> Was falsch ist, wird verkommen
> Obwohl es heut regiert,.
> Was echt ist, das soll kommen—
> Obwohl es heut krepiert. (*G.W.* 8, p. 688)

And people will say/in far away blue days/It will become clear/What is false and what is true/What is false will perish/Although it rules today./What is true shall come—/Although it dies today.

2

The Early Plays

Die Bergbahn (1926–8)

The first version of this play to be performed originally carried the title *Révolte auf Côte 3018* and received its première in Hamburg in November 1927. It was not a success, and Horváth reworked the material, tightening up the structure and transforming the four acts into three, retitling the play *Die Bergbahn* (*The Cable Railway*). As he was to do with many of his later plays, Horváth based this work on actual events. During the construction of the first cable railway on the Zugspitze several workers had been fatally injured and the risks taken by those responsible for the project had showed a callous disregard for loss of human life.*

Since this play illustrates, at least on the surface, a clear conflict between workers and employers (apparent in their use of dialect and Hochdeutsch respectively) it invites comparison with the theme of exploitation which characterizes Brecht's plays, notably *Die Dreigroschenoper* (*The Threepenny Opera*) which received its première in August 1928. Whereas Brecht

---

* In the later novel *Der ewige Spiesser* (1929) Horváth again draws attention to this continuing inhumanity: 'Beide Zugspitzbahnen sind unstreitbar grandiose Spitzenleistungen moderner Bergbahntechnik, und es sind dabei bis Mitte September 1929 schon rund vier Dutzend Arbeiter tödlich verunglückt.' (*G.W. 5*, p. 176) (Both cable railways on the Zugspitze are indisputably magnificent and masterful achievements in modern cable railway technology, and four dozen workers had lost their lives in the process by mid-September 1929). The deliberate use of the conjunction 'und' rather than 'aber' or 'obwohl' is indicative of public indifference rather than Horváth's own.)

had by now evolved an overtly Marxist doctrine that offered a positive political solution (which he hammered home relentlessly!), Horváth's plays suggest no such panacea. Society is portrayed as rotten, it is true, individuals are selfish and hypocritical, but there is little or no intimation that a change in the economic system will improve human nature.

The first victim of the working conditions, Schulz, is a hairdresser from Stettin—scarcely a representative either of the Bavarians or of the working class! Yet he is twice a victim: first at the hands of the brutish worker Moser who savagely attacks him because he has unwittingly made a pass at Moser's girl; secondly when he falls to his death on the following day at work.

Had Horváth wished to write a straight political play on the injustices suffered by the workers, Schulz would hardly have been the first to suffer, but he is clearly meant to be one of the main protagonists since the play opens with his arrival and he is at once marked as an outsider by his speech and background.

This play, the first of the 'Volksstücke', is unique in Horváth's work since it is the only one in which there is a conscious use of dialect. It is also the only play to show traces of Expressionism in the speech of the characters, as well as a somewhat melodramatic use of explosions and the forces of Nature.

Zur schönen Aussicht (1926)

In the same year that he had written *Révolte auf Côte 3018*, Horváth was working on another play which deals less with the broader implications of capitalism and more with the effect of money (or the lack of it) on the individual. Although it anticipates both the tone and the themes of many of his major works, the play remained unperformed until 1969. The hotel, with its ironic name, 'Zur schönen Aussicht' (The Fine Prospect), is a shabby establishment

> am Rande eines mitteleuropäischen Dorfes
>
> on the edge of a mid-European village

and was, according to Horváth's brother, modelled on a small hotel in Murnau. This hotel is peopled by a handful of dubious characters whose backgrounds are all more or less scurrilous, and the suggestion of mutual blackmail is never far away. It is perhaps not surprising that all the male characters are able to unite against the unfortunate Christine when their murky interests are seen to coincide: each one suggests that he has at some time 'had relations' with Christine. The way in which Horváth drives them back on their own accusations when they realize that she has money is a theatrical *tour de force* which creates one of his finest ironic endings. The irony acts as a palliative to one of the nastiest scenes that the author ever wrote.

Exploitation

In each of these plays there is a preoccupation with the idea of exploitation. *Die Bergbahn* shows a group of workers all too aware of the risks they run, their meagre rewards and the glory that accrues to their exploiters, not to mention the financial gain:

> MAURER: Es ist scho a wahr Sünd, was mit die Menschn getriebn wird. Da turnst herum, wie kaum a gewiegter Turist, rackerst di ab mit Lawinen, Steinschlag, Wetter—und was erreichst? Grad, daß dei Essen hast und a Lager, wie a Unterstand, als hätt der Krieg kan End! Abgeschnitten von der Welt. (*Schweigen.*)
> SLIWINSKI: Neulich habens a Ingineur gfeiert.
> MAURER: In der Zeitung is gstanden, er sei unsterbli.
> SIMON: Aber von die Totn schreibt kaner!
> REITER: Die totn san tot.
> OBERLE (*hebt langsam den Kopf*): Die san net tot! Die lebn! (*Schweigen.*)
> SLIWINSKI: Da liest überall vom Fortschritt der

Menschheit und die Leut bekränzn an Ingineur, wie an
Preisstier, die Direkter sperrn die Geldsäck in d'Kass
und dem Bauer blüht der Fremdenverkehr. A jede
Schraubn werd zum 'Wunder der Technik', a jede Odl-
grubn zur 'Heilquelle'. Aber, daß aner sei Lebn
hergebn hat, des Blut werd ausradiert!

SIMON: Na, des werd zu Gold! (Act I, *G.W. 1*, p. 71)

MAURER: It's sinful the way they treat people. You'd hardly see
even the most experienced Alpinist leaping about the way we
do; you battle against avalanches, landslides, weather conditions—and what d'you get for it? Just your food and a camp
like a dug-out, as if the war was still on! Cut off from the rest
of the world. (*Silence*)

SLIWINSKI: Just recently there was a celebration for some
engineer.

MAURER: In the paper they said he was immortal.

SIMON: But no one writes about the dead!

REITER: The dead are dead.

OBERLE (*Slowly raising his head*): They're not dead! They live
on! (*Silence*)

SLIWINSKI: Everywhere you read about the progress of mankind
and people put wreaths round an engineer as if he were a
prize bull, the directors lock up their money-bags in the bank
and the farmers have a blooming tourist trade. Every screw
becomes a 'miracle of technology', every oil-well a 'healing
spring'. But if somebody loses his life the blood is just wiped
away!

SIMON: No, it becomes gold!

This extract from the first act illustrates the mood prevailing
among the men and their awareness of the system for which
they are working. The Christian protestation from Oberle that
the dead are alive has an almost ludicrous and certainly irrele-
vant ring to it; the deaths that follow in the play, his own
included, offer cold comfort in religious terms. In the discussion that ensues Oberle's preaching of non-violence is treated
with scorn by the others:

'Liebe den Kapitalismus wie dich selbst!' (Act I, *G.W.
1*, p. 73)

'Love the capitalist system as thyself'

mocks Simon, and yet Oberle's comments on Moser's treatment of Schulz, telling him that violence produces blood and 'sonst nix' (nothing else), underlined by Schulz's dramatic entry from the storm outside, contain more than a grain of truth. As is so often the case Horváth's sympathies are obvious, an ideology is not. Moser himself is not just a monster and he even tries with his limited powers to explain his actions to Schulz and to apologize:

> Halt!—Du, hör her—i bin extra etwas hint bliebn, weil i di hab sprechn wolln, weil i mit dir hab redn wolln, wegen gestern. Mancher werd halt leicht wütend, des ist Veranlagungssach, net? Verstehst, aber man meints ja gar net so drastisch. Des gestern, des war—horch! I will di net um Verzeihung bittn, i war ja im Recht, verstehst? Wenn da so a Fremder über dei Mensch kimmt, ha? I hab scho ganz recht ghabt! Net? Oder?—Aber da plärrt gleich alls und jeder, man is a Rohling, und man hat do recht, das sakrische Recht is so do auf meiner Seitn, net? Des versteht do jeder!—Aber, weißt, was i net versteh? Daß i im Recht bin und daß es mir trotzdem is, als hätt i Unrecht gtan—verstehst du des? Kann des a Mensch verstehn?! (Act II, *G.W. 1*, p. 79)

> Wait!—Now, listen—I stayed a bit behind specially, because I wanted to speak to you, because I wanted to say something to you. A lot of people get wild easily, it's a matter of temperament, isn't it? But you don't mean it as bad as that, see? That business yesterday, that was—Listen, I don't want to ask you to forgive me, I was right. See? If a stranger like that comes and chats up your bint, eh? I was completely in the right! Wasn't I? Well?—But then everybody starts saying all at once that you're a brute and yet you're in the right. Justice is on my side, isn't it? Anyone can see that!—But, d'you know what I don't understand? That I'm right and yet all the same I feel as if I'd done wrong—d'you understand that? Can anyone understand that?!

Even the Engineer is seen to be exploited and threatened by the company employing him:

> AUFSICHTSRAT: ... Um das Geld nicht zu verlieren, sagt die A.G. 'Hören Sie! Wir haben Ihr Patent erworben. Und die Konzession!'

INGENIEUR: Was soll das?
AUFSICHTSRAT: Aha! Erraten! Es gibt nur wenige A. G.'s
aber zahlreiche Ingenieure. Ingenieure, gleichgültige,
die sich aber auch gerne hetzen ließen, wenn—und
die auch gegen die Arbeiterschaft energischer
einschreiten! Eine Unerhörtheit dieser letzte Streik-
versuch! (Act II, *G.W. 1*, p. 85)

DIRECTOR: In order not to lose money the Company says:
'Listen. We have bought your patent. And the licence!'
ENGINEER: What does that mean?
DIRECTOR: Aha! You've guessed! There are only a few Limited
Companies but there are plenty of engineers. Mediocre
engineers perhaps, but they'd be happy to be pressurized,
if—and they would intervene more vigorously when dealing
with the work force! It was an outrage that last strike attempt!

Zur schönen Aussicht deals with a kind of exploitation that
is no less evident, but it shows characters whose actions are
even more morally reprehensible than those in *Die Bergbahn*.
The setting is the post-war depression and the atmosphere one
of indolent desperation. Strasser, the hotel's proprietor, uses
successive women to support him. Like Max, the chauffeur,
and Franz, the waiter, he has seen better days but now he has
no scruples in using the ageing, alcoholic Ada to help him
maintain a semblance of respectability. The play's action
centres around the men's attempts to exploit Ada and later
Christine for financial motives. It is Ada who dominates the
first half of the play, both as an exploited woman and as one
of the exploiters. She may be seen as a literary forebear
of Dürrenmatt's Claire Zachanassian in *Der Besuch der
alten Dame**; the resemblances in character and speech are
striking:

* In Dürrenmatt's play *Der Besuch der alten Dame* Claire Zachanassian
buys 'justice' (that is Ill's execution) in the following words:
Ich gebe euch eine Milliarde und kaufe mir dafür die Gerechtigkeit.
DER BURGERMEISTER: Wie ist dies zu verstehen, gnädige Frau?
CLAIRE ZACHANASSIAN: Man kann alles kaufen. (Act I)
(I'll give you one thousand million and for that I'll buy myself justice.
THE MAYOR: How are we to interpret this, my lady?
CLAIRE ZACHANASSIAN: One can buy anything.)

ADA: Du bist mein Eigentum, du! Ich habe dich gekauft, und ich kaufe dich jeden Tag! Ich bezahle! (*G.W. 3*, p. 37)

ADA: You are my property! I have bought you and I buy you every day! I pay!

She has none of the grotesque and surreal elements of Dürrenmatt's creation and little of her power. What they do share are the exploitation they have suffered and the relative power that their money now gives them.

God and Mammon

In Horváth's work the phrase 'der liebe Gott' (the good Lord) is used again and again, and yet it is by no means possible to sum up in a few lines what precisely is meant: the interpretation varies from play to play. In negative terms one can say that 'der liebe Gott' is not a conventional deity, although He assumes a variety of more or less terrifying forms and in all the plays preceding *Geschichten aus dem Wiener Wald*, His 'manifestations' are usually associated with money. In act two of *Die Bergbahn*, where the men are working outside in the storm surrounded by snow and glaciers, they hear the thundering sound of falling stones after an explosion and the conversation turns to the Day of Judgement: Hannes maintains that he believes in it, but Simon crudely replies that he'd rather have his arse eaten up by worms than appear before the last judgement since:

Is ja auch nur a Klassengricht! Nebn an gutn Gott spitzelt der Gendarm und dir stellns an Verteidiger, der an sei Schellensolo denkt, net an di! Es gibt kane Gerechtigkeit! (Act II, *G.W. 1*, p. 80)

It's only a judgement according to class! Next to the good Lord there's a policeman informing on you and they give you a defence counsel who's thinking of the sound of his own voice, not about you! There is no justice!

And when Hannes begins to pray after Schulz's death Moser interrupts him in terms reminiscent of Büchner's Woyzeck:

> Verflucht! Ka Litanei, ka Rosenkranz! Der da drobn ist taub für uns arme Leut!
> (*In weiter Ferne Donnerrollen*)
> Ja, donnern, des kann der! Und blitzn und stürmen! Schreckn und vernichten!—was gedeiht, gehört net uns. Was gehört dem armen Mann? Wenn die Sonn scheint, der Staub, wenns regnet, der Dreck. Und allweil Schweiß und Blut ... (Act III, *G.W. 1*, p. 90)

> Damn it! No litanies, no rosaries! Him up there's deaf for us poor people! (*In the far distance thunder.*) Yes, he can make thunder all right. And lightning and storms! Frighten and destroy! Anything that flourishes doesn't belong to us. What does belong to the poor? When the sun shines, dust, and when it rains, mud. And all the time sweat and blood!

In this play at least God, in as much as the characters believe in Him, has some supernatural powers: He is clearly felt in the elements that rage in the mountains; equally clearly He is seen to be on the side of the rich and His powers are used to crush the already oppressed. As the storm grows in intensity so the action reaches its climax with the engineer beginning to shoot wildly at the workers. When he too falls to his death the others help the wounded Moser whose words become increasingly wild and fragmented. He mentions God one final time as the thunder and lightning coincide:

> Holla! Jetzt sprengt der liebe Gott. Da fliegn Staner, Schwererer als Stern—(Act III, *G.W. 1*, p. 95)

> Come on! Now God Himself is exploding. Stones are flying, heavier than stars—

While for the workers in *Die Bergbahn*, God is a threatening, heavenly co-partner in the capitalist system, 'der liebe Gott' becomes altogether more tangible to the characters of *Zur schönen Aussicht*. He is first mentioned by Christine talking to Strasser in act one:

> Es war eine harte Zeit. Ich wurde abgebaut, und wenn der
> liebe Gott mir nicht geholfen hätte, wäre ich
> untergegangen—(*G.W. 3*, p. 26)

> They were hard times. I lost my job and if the good Lord hadn't
> helped me I would have been finished—

A few moments later she repeats that God has helped her, but
it is necessary to the plot for there to be no revelation at this
stage, and so Strasser rather artificially drops his questioning.
The discussion is not picked up again until near the end of act
two:

> STRASSER: Was verstehst du unter 'lieber Gott'?
> CHRISTINE: Zehntausend Mark. (*G.W. 3*, p. 55)

> STRASSER: What do you mean by 'good Lord'?
> CHRISTINE: Ten thousand Marks.

Christine is the first of several Horváth characters for whom
the phrase 'der liebe Gott' means a windfall. In the play *Rund
um den Kongreß* (1928–9),* Horváth carries the 'lieber Gott'
motif to even greater extremes. Money has so much usurped
the place of God in men's minds that he becomes a unit of
currency which can be broken down. The following farcical
but grotesque exchanges take place:

> ALFRED: ... Was machst du mit deinem lieben Gott?
> FERDINAND: Privatisieren.
> ALFRED: Du könntest deinen lieben Gott verdoppeln.
> (*G.W. 3*, p. 92)

> ALFRED: What are you doing with your good Lord?
> FERDINAND: Living on my private means.
> ALFRED: You could double your good Lord.

and

> FERDINAND: Ich hab mir nämlich gedacht, daß vielleicht
> vorerst der halbe liebe Gott reichen könnte, dürfte,

* Many of this play's ideas and whole passages of dialogue have been
transposed from *Zur schönen Aussicht* while other are to be found in *Geschichten aus dem Wiener Wald*, notably the words of Luise Gift, some of which
appear virtually unchanged in Marianne's mouth.

müßte, sollte ... (*Ferdinand gibt ihm den halben lieben Gott ...*)

ALFRED: ... Endlich Luft. Als kleiner Kaufmann erwürgt dich die Konkurrenz, aber schon mit einem halben lieben Gott in der Tasche kann man an die Gründung eines Konzerns—(*G.W. 3*, p. 108)

> FERDINAND: Actually I thought that perhaps initially half of the good Lord could, might, would have to, ought to suffice ... (*Ferdinand gives him half the good Lord.*)
> ALFRED: ... I can breathe at last. As a small trader you're stifled by competition, but even with half a good Lord in your pocket setting up a business can be—

It is a sign of the times that people should see money as being the manifestation of God on earth. The image is pushed even further by Christine at the end of the play:

> Es gibt einen lieben Gott, aber auf den ist kein Verlaß. Er hilft nur ab und zu, die meisten, dürfen verrecken. Man müßte den lieben Gott besser organisieren. Man könnte ihn zwingen. Und dann auf ihn verzichten. (*G.W. 3*, p. 73)

> There is a God but there's no counting on Him. He only helps out now and again, most people can just rot. God ought to be better organized. You could bring Him under control. And then give Him up.

Even before Christine had appeared in act one, Müller had congratulated Strasser on his

> außerordentlich vorteilhaften Vertrag mit dem lieben Gott

> extraordinarily advantageous contract with the good Lord

an ironic reference to the weather which seems to change to suit Strasser's purposes; ironic too in the very different meaning it will assume later in the play! Another instance where God is mentioned (and here it is significantly the one word 'Gott' rather than 'der liebe Gott') is in the second act when Christine is being vilified by the men in order to extricate Strasser from any responsibility for her and her child. Here there is no irony intended by Horváth:

> Jetzt weiß ich nicht mehr, ob es einen Gott gibt. Wenn ich nur verzweifeln könnte. (*G.W. 3*, p. 52)
>
> Now I don't know any more whether there's a God or not. If only I could just despair.

Here it is the overwhelming force of evil around her that seems to negate the possibility of any divinity.

Humour in *Zur schönen Aussicht*

Even in the play *Hin und her* (*To and fro*) which Horváth called a 'Posse' (farce) the underlying motif is a serious one. What differentiates the 'Komödien' (comedies) from the 'Schauspiele' (dramas) and the 'Volksstücke' (folk-plays) is above all their endings and much less their comic elements. The outcome in the 'Schauspiele' is irredeemably tragic; in the 'Volksstücke' there are examples both of mock happy endings and unambiguously grim ones; the 'Komödien' are without exception plays where solutions (however contrived they may be!) are found to the problems. Christine is 'victorious' at the end of *Zur schönen Aussicht* for example, but this is only possible because of her inheritance.

The comedy in all of Horváth's plays derives mainly from the stupidity of the characters, often coupled with an irony of situation. Thus in *Zur schönen Aussicht* the most comic dialogue comes in the final act where all the men are desperately trying to woo Christine's money. Max comes to her with the most preposterous 'confession':

> ... Vielleicht drücke ich mich ungeschickt aus, aber es ist so. Lachen Sie mich nicht aus, bitte. Wir zwei müssen uns schon begegnet sein, da ich Sie nicht vergessen kann. Ja, wir haben uns sogar schon geliebt, in unserer letzten Inkarnation, ich bin nämlich Buddhist. Vor tausend Jahren waren Sie ein Ritter und ich war Ihr treuer Knappe. (*G.W. 3*, p. 68)
>
> Perhaps I'm expressing myself rather clumsily but that's how it is. Please don't laugh at me. We two must have met in the past

since I can't forget you. Yes, we even loved one another in our
last incarnation. I'm a Buddhist you see. A thousand years ago
you were a knight and I was your faithful vassal.

Another example of a far blacker humour is where the
contrast between the inflated language (with the accompanying music), and the grotesquely inappropriate behaviour of
the partners is abruptly unmasked:

ADA: ... Sag: liebst du mich?
KARL (*rülpst*): Ja.
ADA: Aber nicht nur meinen Leib, meine Reize—auch
    meine Seele, nicht?
KARL: Auch deine Seele.
(*Irgendwo singt eine Geige Schmachtfetzen*)
ADA: Ist das schön du—du starker, großer, du Siegfried!
    Und dann regnet es auch nicht mehr, die Sterne stehen
    am Himmel—wenn ich nicht nur so dürstig wäre!
    Durst! Durst! Ist das die Sehnsucht?
KARL: Nein, das ist Durst.
(*Die Geige hat ausgesungen*)
ADA (*reisst sich los von Karl*): Pfui! Jetzt war ich wieder
    sentimental, was? (Act I, *G.W. 3*, p. 29–30)

ADA: ... Tell me: do you love me?
KARL (*Belching*): Yes.
ADA: But not only my body, my charms—you love my soul too,
    don't you?
KARL: Your soul too.
(*Somewhere a violin is playing languid snatches of tune*)
ADA: Isn't that beautiful, you—you great strong Siegfried, you!
    And it's not raining any more, there are stars in the sky—If
    only I weren't so thirsty! Thirst! Thirst! Is that a yearning?
KARL: No, that's thirst.
(*The sound of the violin has died away*)
ADA (*Pulling herself away from Karl*): Bah! I was being senti-
    mental again, wasn't I?

Humour in Horváth's work is seldom of the knock-about
variety; beneath the comic lines, the ironic situations, there
are almost always ulterior motives, hypocrisy and an abyss of
stupidity.

3

The Political Plays

The background

In both *Sladek der schwarze Reichswehrmann* (*Sladek the Black Militiaman*) and *Italienische Nacht* (*Italian Night*) it is political rather than economic circumstances that form the background. Sladek was a reworking of the earlier play *Sladek oder die schwarze Armee* (*Sladek or the Black Army*), omitting the court scene and Sladek's flight, and dropping the device of using one actor for three roles (the Government official, the policeman and the judge were all played by the same actor), a device which had the effect of suggesting a character type rather than individuals. This play was written while Horváth was working with the 'Deutsche Liga für Menschenrechte' (German League for Human Rights) whose work frequently involved investigations into the activities of the secret right-wing paramilitary groups who took it into their hands to mete out 'justice'. Such groups were not only tolerated: successive governments of the Weimar Republic were notoriously lax in punishing their crimes. Indeed in those quiet country towns where Black Army members did go on trial they escaped with ludicrously light sentences and there seems to have been a clear connection between the Black Army and the official 'Reichswehr'. Certainly this kind of collaboration is strongly implied in both the *Sladek* plays.

Italienische Nacht has an even more personal slant to it since, after writing the play, Horváth saw a similar 'Saalschlacht' and he also testified subsequently at the trial.

Coming after his unflattering portrayal of the Nazis in *Sladek* it ensured his place on their list of politically suspect writers. The breaking up of any kind of socialist political gathering was a tactic commonly employed by the Nazi Party, and it was not many years before the relative complacency of the moderate socialists was to have disastrous results: their mildness and self-satisfaction left the door wide open to the brutal efficiency of the extreme Right.

The individual in the movement

Sladek and Anna

While both plays appear to be about politics it is important to see where the centre of gravity really lies in each. Only on the surface is Horváth writing about rival political factions and their ideological (or physical) battles. Of Sladek he wrote:

> Sladek ist als Figur ein völlig aus unserer Zeit geborener und nur durch sie erklärbarer Typ; er ist, wie ein Berliner Verleger ihn einmal nannte, eine Gestalt, die zwischen Büchners Wozzeck und dem Schwejk liegt. Ein ausgesprochener Vertreter jener Jugend, jenes Jahrgangs 1902, der in seiner Pubertät die 'große Zeit', Krieg und Inflation, mitgemacht hat, er ist der Typus des Traditionslosen, Entwurzelten, dem jedes feste Fundament fehlt und der so zum Prototyp des Mitläufers wird. Ohne eigentlich Mörder zu sein, begeht er einen Mord. Ein pessimistischer Sucher, liebt er die Gerechtigkeit—ohne daß er an sie glaubt, er hat keinen Boden, keine Front ... Die inhaltliche Form meines Stückes ist historisches Drama, denn die Vorgänge sind bereits historisch geworden. Aber seine Idee, seine Tendenz ist ganz heutig. Ich glaube, daß ein wirklicher Dramatiker kein Wort ohne Tendenz schreiben kann. Es kommt nur darauf an, ob sie ihm bewußt wird oder nicht. Allerdings lehne ich durchaus die dichterische Schwarz-Weiß-Zeichnung, auch im sozialen Drama, ab. Da ich die Hauptprobleme der Menschheit in erster Linie von sozialen Gesichtspunkten aus sehe, kam es mir bei meinem *Sladek* vor allem darauf

an, die gesellschaftlichen Kräfte aufzuzeigen, aus denen
dieser Typus entstanden ist. (*G.W. 2*, pp. 663–4)

As a figure Sladek is completely a child of our time and can only
be explained by that fact; he is, as one Berlin publisher
described him, a character who stands between Büchner's Woz-
zeck and Schweyk. He is decidedly a representative of the youth
of 1902 which experienced in its puberty the 'great age', war and
inflation; he is the typical example of those without roots and
traditions, lacking any firm basis and so becoming the prototype
of the time-server. Without really being a murderer he commits
a murder. He is a pessimistic seeker who loves justice—without
believing in it. The form of my play is historical drama since the
events have already become historical. But the idea and the bias
in it are entirely contemporary. I believe that a true dramatist
cannot write one word without bias. It just depends on whether
he is conscious of it or not. Certainly I utterly reject black and
white portraits, even in social drama. Since I consider the main
problems of mankind from a social standpoint in the first
instance my main concern in *Sladek* was to show the forces in
society which have brought about the emergence of this type.

The above does not of course make Sladek merely a victim of
circumstances: he too could act differently and he could think
for himself before joining the Black Army, but it is far more
appealing to belong, to be part of an organization that seems
itself to be part of a historical process. In this way the problem
of individual responsibility is thrust away beneath the protective banner of Fascism. The use of Nazi songs in the play shows
how effectively men are united in hatred and blood-lust (a
theme taken up again in Horváth's last novel *Ein Kind unserer
Zeit* (*A Child of our Time*)). Nowhere is this more true than
at the end of the play when Sladek dies with the poignant
appeal:

Ich bitte mich als Menschen zu betrachten und nicht als
Zeit. (*G.W. 2*, p. 527)

I ask you to consider me as a human being and not as (the
representative of) an era.

To this the final answer is a rousing rendering of *Deutschland,
Deutschland über alles.*

When he first begins to talk to Schminke (who, as his name, 'make-up', implies, wears his Marxism as a mask)* Sladek again and again uses the word 'denken' (to think); he stresses the importance of thinking for oneself; the need to come to one's own conclusions:

> Ich denk viel. Ich denk den ganzen Tag. (Act I, *G. W. 2*, p. 488)
>
> I think a lot. I think the whole day long.

His identification with the Fatherland and his endless clichés show how just the opposite is true. His speech is marked by repetition and his catch-phrase is:

> In der Natur wird gemordet, das ändert sich nicht. (Act I, *G.W. 2*, p. 489)
>
> Killing is part of nature and that doesn't change.

It is only at the end when he is going to his own death that Sladek uses the phrase in a context where it comes alive and is all too appropriate. The 'großes Gesetz' of which he has spoken without comprehension has now caught up with him.

Once again it is a woman, Anna, who is the first victim. She is fifteen years older than Sladek and, like Valerie in *Geschichten aus dem Wiener Wald*, she clings desperately to Sladek and, being less wordly-wise than Valerie, she tries to prevent him from going with the Black Army:

> Ich bitte Sie, lassen Sie mir den Sladek. Es fällt mir schwer darüber zu reden. Wenn sich eine Frau in meinem Alter an einem fünfzehn Jahre jüngeren Mann hängt, so ist das immer mütterlich, und sie läßt ihn nicht aus den Augen. Sladek ist noch ein Junge, der sich an nichts erinnern kann als an den Krieg. Er kann sich den Frieden gar nicht vorstellen, so mißtrauisch ist er. Er ist in der großen Zeit

---

* It has been pointed out by writers who were living in Berlin in the twenties that a Communist Dr Schmincke—a respected and well-known figure—would undoubtedly have been known to Horváth. Even if this was the case the character in *Sladek* should not be taken as a model of political and moral uprightness: Horváth was never given to creating such characters!

groß geworden, das merkt man. Ich lasse ihn nicht aus
den Augen, ich habe gehorcht und spioniert—mich kann
man nämlich nicht betrügen. Was mein ist, bleibt mein.
(Act 1, *G.W. 2*, p. 499)

I beg you to leave Sladek with me. It's hard for me to talk about
it. When a woman of my age clings to a man who's fifteen years
younger, then she's always like a mother and she doesn't let him
out of her sight. Sladek is still a boy who can't remember
anything except war. He's so mistrustful that he can't even
imagine peace. He grew up in the Great Age, you can see that. I
don't let him out of my sight. I've done my eavesdropping and
spying—people just can't deceive me. What is mine remains
mine.

and:

Bitte, sagen Sie dem Sladek kein Wort, daß ich weiß, daß
er von mir will. Bitte, sagen Sie ihm doch, er wäre zum
Soldaten untauglich, sagen Sie es ihm, bitte lassen Sie ihn
hier. Ihre Soldaten werden auch ohne Sladek mars-
chieren, aber ich—Ich hab schon mal alles für das Vater-
land geopfert. Ich laß mir nichts mehr rauben. Ich verrate
die ganze Armee den Polen. Noch heut. (Act I, *G.W. 2*, p.
500)

Please don't tell Sladek that I know he wants to get away
from me. Please tell him he's not fit for service as a soldier,
tell him that, please leave him here. Your soldiers can march
without Sladek, but me—I've already sacrificed everything
for the fatherland. I won't let myself be robbed of anything
else. I'll betray the whole army to the Poles. And I'll do it
today.

Anna acts not out of cunning but out of desperation; Sladek
out of self-interest tempered with guilt, and later with the
realization of what he has lost and of the wrong that he has
done. Needless to say the realization comes too late to save
Anna but in time to destroy himself: after betraying Anna he
realizes that all her threats were idle ones, designed only to
keep him away from the Black Army and he cries 'Halt' in an
attempt to stop her murder:

SALM: Hände hoch! Was sollte das Halt?
SLADEK: Weil sie unschuldig war.
SALM: Das gibt es nicht.
SLADEK: Doch.
SALM: Seit wann?
SLADEK: Seit zwei Minuten ...
SLADEK: ... Ich hab nur an die Gerechtigkeit gedacht. Es war mir plötzlich, als wären meine Ansichten über die Natur falsch und ich hätt die Wahrheit vergessen. Ich kann nämlich selbstständig denken—
SALM (*unterbricht ihn*): Du hast nicht selbständig zu denken! Du bist Soldat. (Act II, *G.W. 2*, p. 513)

SALM: Hands up! What did that stop mean?
SLADEK: Because she was innocent.
SALM: That's not true.
SLADEK: Yes it is.
SALM: Since when?
SLADEK: Two minutes ago ...
SLADEK: ... I was only thinking of justice. It suddenly seemed as though my views of nature were wrong, as if I had forgotten the truth. I can think for myself you see—
SALM (*interrupting him*): It's not your job to think for yourself! You're a soldier.

When confronted with the reconstruction of events at the end of the play Sladek can only say:

Das ist sehr kompliziert (*G.W. 2*, p. 526)

That's very complicated

as Schminke explains Anna's death as a political murder, and the Secretary of State (who has come with the regular 'Reichswehr' to cover up all traces of the Black Army) describes it as the bestial act of a frustrated man who had been exploiting an ageing woman and no longer been able to get the money that he wanted from her. The Marxist Schminke, whose phrase-making is only marginally preferable to that of the Nazis, says that he will remain a terrorist because 'Ich muß' (I have to). Sladek, the only person who has come to some realization during the play, repeats the words:

Das hab ich auch schon gehört. Das hab ich auch schon
gehört (*G.W. 2*, p. 527)

Yes, I've heard that too. Yes, I've heard that too.

Will the acts that may be perpetrated by Schminke be any
more noble and any more helpful to the cause of justice than
those in which Sladek has been involved? Do the slogans
of the opposing factions sound so very different? Horváth's
plea is not for passive acceptance of the inevitable but for a
lucid, critical awareness that can see through slogans and
lies.

The Women in Italienische Nacht
Sladek had been set in the camp of the Nazis and had shown
their internal conflicts; *Italienische Nacht*, while dealing with
two political groups (Republicans, i.e. socialists, and Nazis)
centres around the discussions and actions of the Republicans,
beginning and ending with them. The town councillor's words
at the opening of the play:

Von einer akuten Bedrohung der demokratischen
Republik kann natürlich keineswegs gesprochen werden.
Schon weil es der Reaktion an einem ideologischen
Unterbau mangelt. (*G.W. 1*, p. 103)

There can be no talk about an acute threat to the democratic
republic. And that is because the reactionary forces have no
ideological foundations.

and their exact repetition at the end show how entrenched the
Republicans are in their card-playing, beer-swilling complacency, just as the Black Army are in their fanatical hatred. In
this way the two plays complement each other and justify
Horváth's statement about writing 'gegen die Masse der
Politisierenden' (see Introduction). The play has not the personal tragedies of *Sladek der schwarze Reichswehrmann* but it
is once again a woman (Adele, wife of the boorish councillor)
who shows both love and common sense. At first she appears
to be a somewhat tragi-comic figure who is treated brutally by

her husband and 'allowed out' once or twice a year in his company:

> BETZ: Ich habe dich mal mit ihr gehen sehen.
> STADTRAT: Mich? Mit ihr? Wir gehen doch nie zusammen aus.
> BETZ: Doch. Und zwar dürft das so vor Weihnachten gewesen sein.
> STADTRAT: Richtig! Das war an ihrem Geburtstag! Der einzige Tag im Jahr, an dem sie mitgehen darf, ins Kino—(Bild V, *G.W. 1*, p. 129)

> BETZ: I once saw you walking with her.
> COUNCILLOR: Me? With her? But we never go out together!
> BETZ: Yes, you were. And it must have been just before Christmas.
> COUNCILLOR: You're right! That was on her birthday! The only time of the year she's allowed to go with me, to the cinema—

Yet their thirty years of marriage suddenly galvanize Adele to action when the Fascist major insults her husband; and her words—that finally put the Nazis to flight—show more humanity than has been expressed by all the other characters in the play taken together:

> Halten Sie Ihr Maul! Und ziehen Sie sich das Zeug da aus, der Krieg ist doch endlich vorbei, Sie Hanswurst! Verzichtens lieber auf Ihre Pension zugunsten der Kriegskrüppel und arbeitens mal was Anständiges, anstatt arme Menschen in ihren Gartenunterhaltungen zu stören, Sie ganz gewöhnlicher Schweinhund! (Bild VII, *G.W. 1*, p. 156)

> Shut your mouth! And take off that nonsense you're wearing, the war's over now, you clown! Why don't you hand over your pension for the cripples of the war and do a decent job of work instead of disturbing poor people who're having a chat in a café garden, you common swine!

The major and his men depart, and one is left with the impression that Adele has spoken the only words in the play which have both the ring of sincerity and a practical application. That such words are enough to conquer Fascism is a more doubtful hypothesis.

Once again in this play it is the women who talk both with more sensitivity and with more insight than the men. It is Leni for example who comments on the 'Herren in Uniform' (gentlemen in uniform):

> Die sehn sich alle so fad gleich (Bild II, *G.W.1*, p. 109)
>
> they all look so alike in their dullness.

It is Anna who infiltrates the Fascist camp and finds out what they are planning and who sees the risk of fragmenting their own party if the Fascists are allowed to break up the Italienische Nacht:

> Ich würde ihnen schon helfen, sie stehens uns doch immer noch näher als die anderen. (Bild VI, *G.W. 1*, p. 141)
>
> I would help them, they are closer to us than the others in any event.

The men on the other hand are seen playing cards, drinking, insulting their wives and exchanging hollow phrases; at best they show verbal aggression for their opponents, and the extreme left daub a statue of the Kaiser with red paint—hardly an act likely to advance the cause of peace and reason! The militant Martin pulls out the kind of clichés on history that are no more helpful than Sladek's 'großes Gesetz':

> Die historischen Gesetze kümmern sich einen Dreck um Privatschicksale, sie schreiten unerbittlich über den einzelnen hinweg, und zwar vorwärts. (Bild VI, *G.W. 1*, p. 140)
>
> The laws of History don't give a damn about individual destinies, they march relentlessly over the individual and they march onwards.

In each case it is left to the women to think of individual destiny and this they do mostly with a spirit of generosity and self-sacrifice.

Stupidity, hypocrisy and self-deception

As must be apparent to any student of Horváth's plays, characters are more often than not generously endowed with these three qualities. Indeed their conversation would in many cases become non-existent without them. In *Sladek* it is firstly the violent language of racial hatred that strikes the audience—'Judenknecht' (Jew-server), 'Syphilitische Neger' (syphilitic niggers), 'jüdisch-jesuitische Fetzen von Weimar' (Jewish-Jesuitical tatters from Weimar); in *Italienische Nacht* it is the self-satisfied utterances on the strength of the Weimar Republic and the weakness of the Fascists. The political slogan-mongering that Horváth so roundly condemned is illustrated on page after page in both plays.

On another level there are 'intellectual' discussions: between Sladek and Schminke, Betz and Martin. In these the characters are seen playing with half-digested ideas. In the case of Sladek and Schminke it is the role of the individual in society. Sladek is so indoctrinated with the ideals of Fascism that he is even able to answer the question

> Was verstehst du unter Vaterland?

with

> Zu guter Letzt mich.
> (Act I, *G.W. 2*, p. 489)

> What do you mean by fatherland? When it comes down to it—myself,

adding a few lines later that he can think for himself! His 'thoughts' run along these lines:

> Es wird bald alles eine Stadt, das ganze deutsche Reich. Wir brauchen unsere Kolonien wieder, Asien, Afrika—wir sind wirklich zu viel. Schad, daß der Krieg aus ist! (Act I, *G.W. 2*, p. 490)

> Soon everything will be one town, the whole German Reich. We need our colonies again, Asia, Africa—there are really too many of us. Pity that the war's over!

('Why we need colonies' was later to become the title for a Geography essay in *Jugend ohne Gott*.) In *Italienische Nacht* the discussion on Freud leads to this delightful conclusion:

> Ich kann dir sagen, daß unsere Aggressionstriebe eine direkt überragende Rolle bei der Verwirklichung des Sozialismus spielen. Ich fürcht, daß du in diesem Punkte eine Vogel-Strauß-Politik treibst. (Bild II, *G.W. 1, p. 113*)

> I can tell you that our aggressive urges play a predominant role in the realization of Socialism. I fear that in this respect you are being a political ostrich.

The underlying truth of Betz's assertion is made comic not only by Martin's obscene rejoinders but also by his own pomposity in presenting the argument and his undigested regurgitation of it.

The third and most prevalent form of stupidity lies in the ordinary conversation of the characters. When Sladek is found by Anna (just after he has paid a barmaid to strip for him) he tries to convince her of his desire to return to her; in fact he is preparing the ground for her murder:

> SLADEK: Anna—. Ich wollte wieder zu dir kommen.
> ANNA (*starrt ihn entsetzt an*): Das ist nicht wahr!
> SLADEK: Doch.
> ANNA (*sieht sich ängstlich um*): Wo warst du?
> SLADEK: Bei den Soldaten. Ich hab mir das alles überlegt.
> ANNA: Was willst du von mir?—Was denkst du jetzt?
> SLADEK: Daß alles wieder gut wird.
> ANNA: Das gibt es nicht.
> SLADEK: Ich hab dich lieb.
> ANNA: Nein. Nein.
> SLADEK: Ich lüge nicht.
> ANNA: Heut abend hättest du mich erschlagen können.
> SLADEK: Ich hab dich nie gehaßt. (Act II, *G.W. 2*, p. 512)

> SLADEK: Anna—. I wanted to come back to you.
> ANNA (*looking at him in horror*): That's not true!
> SLADEK: Yes it is.
> ANNA (*looking round anxiously*): Where were you?

SLADEK: With the soldiers. I've thought it all over.
ANNA: What do you want from me? What are you thinking now?
SLADEK: That everything'll be all right.
ANNA: That's impossible.
SLADEK: I'm fond of you.
ANNA: No. No.
SLADEK: I'm not lying.
ANNA: This very evening you could've killed me.
SLADEK: I've never hated you.

Sladek, the 'independent' thinker is merely repeating in colourless fashion what Knorke has told him to say. The irony in this absurd piece of hypocrisy is that Anna, the one person in the play who has genuine emotions and shows them, finally makes Sladek realize that he *did* care for her, but only when it is too late.

Horváth was a master at portraying the inconsequential leaps that occur in everyday conversations, especially where characters are trying to impress one another. In this he leaves behind the drama of carefully constructed, logical development in dialogue and anticipates the post-war dramatists who have taken the absurdities of speech to its extremes. Horváth's writing is no parody and the inconsequentialities, however comic they may be, always remain credible; each character follows his train of thought, drops his cliché or *bon mot* into the ring and—just occasionally—says what he is really thinking:

STADTRAT: Wenn du zum Weibe gehst, vergiß die Peitsche nicht.
BETZ: Das ist von Nietzsche.
STADTRAT: Das ist mir wurscht! Sie folgt aufs Wort. Das ist doch ein herrlicher Platz hier! Diese uralten Stämme und die ozonreiche Luft—(*Er atmet tief*)
BETZ: Das sind halt die Wunder der Natur.
STADTRAT: Die Wunder der Schöpfung—es gibt nichts Herrlicheres. Ich kann das besser beurteilen, weil ich ein Bauernkind bin. Wenn man so in den Himmel schaut, kommt man sich so winzig vor—diese ewigen Sterne! Was sind wir daneben?

BETZ: Nichts.

STADTRAT: Nichts. Gott hat doch einen feinen Geschmack.

BETZ: Es ist halt alles relativ.

(*Stille*)

STADTRAT: Du, Betz, ich hab mir ein Gründstück gekauft.

(*G.W. 1*, p. 131)

COUNCILLOR: When you go to a woman, don't forget the whip.

BETZ: That's Nietzsche.

COUNCILLOR: And damn all I care! She obeys me to the letter. This is a glorious spot here! These age-old tree trunks and the air filled with ozone—(*he takes a deep breath*)

BETZ: Those are the wonders of nature.

COUNCILLOR: The wonders of creation—there's nothing more glorious. I can judge that better than you because I was born on a farm. When you look up into the sky, you seem so tiny in comparison—those eternal stars! What are we next to them?

BETZ: Nothing.

COUNCILLOR: Nothing. God really has got good taste.

BETZ: Everything's relative of course.

(*Silence*)

COUNCILLOR: You know what, Betz, I've bought myself a piece of land.

A conversation between Karl and Leni shows how self-deception leads to an absurd inflation of language and, as in *Zur schönen Aussicht*, heart-strings and purse-strings are plucked simultaneously: nothing is so sure to quicken the emotions as the mention of cash! Once again God is the starting point, but Leni and Karl are not really talking of religion any more than they are talking of love. Karl's self-pitying defeatism is treated with tenderness and understanding by Leni (who makes some of the most pertinent comments in the play), but she too succumbs here to an illusion:

LENI: Glaubst du an Gott? (*Karl schweigt*). Es gibt einen, und es gibt auch eine Erlösung.

KARL: Wenn ich nur wüßt, wer mich verflucht hat.

LENI: Laß mich dich erlösen.

KARL: Du? Mich?

LENI: Ich hab viertausend Mark, und wir gründen eine Kolonialwarenhandlung—
KARL: Wir?
LENI: Draußen bei meinem Onkel—
KARL: Wir?
LENI: Ich und du.
(*Stille*)
KARL: In bar?
LENI: Ja.
(*Stille*)
KARL: Was denkst du jetzt? Denkst du jetzt an eine Ehegemeinschaft? Nein, dazu bist du mir zu schad!
LENI: Oh, Mann, sprich doch nicht so hartherzig! Ich kenn dich ja schon durch und durch, wenn ich dich auch erst seit kurz kenn! (*Sie wirft sich ihm an den Hals; große Kußszene*)
KARL: Ich hab ja schon immer von der Erlösung durch das Weib geträumt, aber ich habs halt nicht glauben können—ich bin nämlich sehr verbittert, weißt du?
LENI (*gibt ihm einen Kuß auf die Stirn*): Ja, die Welt ist voll Neid. (*G.W. 1*, p. 144–5)*

LENI: Do you believe in God? (*Karl is silent*) There is a God and there is a salvation too.
KARL: If only I knew who had put a curse on me.
LENI: Let me be your salvation.
KARL: You? My salvation?
LENI: I have four thousand Marks and we'll set up a grocery shop—
KARL: We?
LENI: Out at my uncle's.
KARL: Wc?
LENI: Me and you.
(*Silence*)
KARL: In cash?
LENI: Yes.
(*Silence*)
KARL: What are you thinking now? Are you thinking of a business marriage? No, you're too good for that!
LENI: Don't be so hard-hearted! I know you through and through already although I've only known you for a short

_____
* There is, of course, in this scene an ironic echo of Goethe: Leni's question 'Glaubst du an Gott?' recalls Gretchen's in *Faust I*, 'Marthens Garten.'

while. (*She throws her arms round his neck—big kissing scene*)

KARL: I've always dreamed of salvation coming through a woman, but I've never been able to believe it possible—I'm very embittered, you know.

LENI (*giving him a kiss on the forehead*): Yes, the world is full of envy.

Language—and especially the language of 'Bildungsjargon' (dealt with in the next chapter)—is a cover, a mask that conceals true feelings. More often than not it is in the silences that the real thoughts of the characters are revealed, while their words merely serve to give a semblance of continuity and of communication in relationships where none exists.

4

Geschichten aus dem Wiener Wald

The background, the music and the motto

The title and the eponymous waltz which is heard at the opening and at the end of *Geschichten aus dem Wiener Wald* (1930–1) (*Tales from the Vienna Woods*) as if played by 'ein himmlisches Streichorchester' (a heavenly string orchestra) and played jerkily on the piano by a schoolgirl during the play, conjure up images of an idyll. The expectations aroused all suggest a mood of carefree happiness set in and around the Austrian capital. As a background for the shabby characters and sordid events from their everyday life Horváth wanted to make sure that he created the Vienna that people imagined to be the true one: the Vienna Woods, the Danube, the Wine Festival, the music of Johann Strauss. Between such a background and the action of the play the contrast could hardly be more extreme, and in his synthesis of the two Horváth is able to unmask not only his characters but the comfortable myth of Vienna with which both characters and spectators live.

There are more than forty musical items in the play (twelve in part I, only seven in part II and over twenty in part III). Almost all of them have a distinctly Viennese flavour, whether it be the halting progress of the waltzes played on the piano by a schoolgirl that accompany the scenes in the 'Stille Straße im achten Bezirk' (quiet street in Vienna 8) or the traditional drinking songs that open part III. The music is used very precisely: at times it is designed to create a mood, at others to contrast with the action; frequently it is broken off to emphasize an exact moment in conversation, a sudden silence or a spiteful comment:

> (*Der Rittmeister vertieft sich in die Ziehungsliste; plötzlich bricht der Walzer ab, mitten im Takt*)
> VALERIE (*schadenfroh*): Was haben wir denn gewonnen, Herr Rittmeister? Das große Los? (Act I, sc 2, *G.W. 1*, p. 167)

> (*The captain buries himself in the list of lottery results; the waltz suddenly breaks off in mid-phrase*)
> VALERIE (*maliciously*): And what have we won, then, captain? The big prize?

As well as the piano and the various orchestral pieces the play also includes a portable gramophone which provides 'culture' in the form of a Puccini aria at the picnic, a lute in the inappropriate hands of Oskar, and, most masterful of all, a zither, the frailest instrument, in the hands of the grandmother who plays it with malicious triumph as Marianne collapses at the end of the play.

The play's motto is:

> Nichts gibt so sehr das Gefühl der Unendlichkeit als wie die Dummheit (*G.W. 1*, p. 157)

> Nothing gives so strong an impression of infinity as stupidity.

and this is the key to the circle of events in the play. With the exception of the grandmother* (probably Horváth's most pernicious creation) there are no villains in the play who cause the tragedy; the protagonists all have a recognizable streak of humanity that prevents our total alienation from them and

---

* In an undated short story *Großmütterleins Tod* (*Granny's Death*) there is a similarly evil septuagenarian grandmother whose actions and apparent frailty parallel those of Alfred's grandmother. Her aim is to bring about strife and ultimately separation between her son and his pregnant wife (she is given the homely title 'Großmütterlein' as soon as they know that she is a granny-to-be). When she succeeds in her aim it seems as though Horváth relented, since in this case it is she who sits in a draught, catches pneumonia and dies, realizing the evil of her ways.

their stupidity, a stupidity that is at times wilful and at times beyond their understanding.

The language

Any reader of a Horváth play will immediately be struck by the number of instances where the word 'Stille' (silence) is used as a stage direction. He will wonder how and with what effect such pauses can be acted out on stage. Horváth wrote in his *Gebrauchsanweisung* (Directions for Use—a term found on medicine bottles):

> Bitte achten Sie genau auf die Pausen im Dialog, die ich mit 'Stille' bezeichne—hier kämpft das Bewußtsein oder Unterbewußtsein miteinander, und das muß sichtbar werden. (*G.W. 8*, p. 664)
>
> Please pay close attention to the pauses in the dialogue that I have marked 'Silence'—here conscious or subconscious ideas are in conflict and that must become visible.

These pauses must therefore be long enough for the spectator not to be carried along by the flow of the conversation; he must, in an almost Brechtian sense, feel outside the action and consider the implications. But unlike the Brechtian spectator he shares this moment with the characters on stage.

The finest example of this device is seen when Alfred visits his mother and grandmother for the second time:

DIE GROßMUTTER: Bist ein armer Teufel, lieber Alfred—
ALFRED: Warum?
DIE GROßMUTTER: Daß du immer solchen Weibern in die Händ fallen mußt—
(*Stille*)
Du, Alfred. Wenn du dich jetzt von deinem Marianderl trennst, dann tät ich dir was leihen—
ALFRED: Wieso?
DIE GROßMUTTER: Hast mich nicht verstanden?
(*Stille*)
ALFRED: Wieviel?
DIE GROßMUTTER: Bist doch noch jung und schön—

ALFRED (*deutet auf den Kinderwagen*): Und das dort?
DIE GROßMUTTER: An das denk jetzt nicht. Fahr nur mal
   fort—
(*Stille*)
ALFRED: Wohin?
DIE GROßMUTTER: Nach Frankreich. Dort gehts jetz noch
   am besten, hab ich in der Zeitung gelesen.—Wenn ich
   jung wär, ich tät sofort nach Frankreich—(Act II, sc 5,
   G.W. 1, pp. 208–9)

GRANDMOTHER: Poor unfortunate devil, you are, Alfred—
ALFRED: Why?
GRANDMOTHER: Because you're always falling into the clutches
   of women like that—
(*Silence*)
ALFRED: If you leave your precious Marianne, I'll lend you some
   money.
(*Silence*)
ALFRED: What?
GRANDMOTHER: Haven't you understood?
(*Silence*)
ALFRED: How much?
GRANDMOTHER: You're still young and handsome—
ALFRED (*Points at the pram*): What about that?
GRANDMOTHER: Don't think about that. Just go away some-
   where—
(*Silence*)
ALFRED: Where?
GRANDMOTHER: France. Everything's still going well over there I
   read in the paper. If I were young, I'd be off to France straight
   away—

Considering the previous scene where Marianne has been sold
into the night club world by her loving Alfred—scarcely the
victim of 'women like that'—there is good reason for a pause.
The second 'Stille' comes at the moment when a particularly
insidious bribe is implied, despite the use of the affectionate
diminutive 'Marianderl'. The third 'Stille' shows how the old
woman's calculations are being pondered by Alfred whose
sole response when offered money to leave Marianne is 'How
much?'. In the final instance the horror can only be
appreciated in retrospect: 'das dort', the fruit of their love,

also has a part in the grandmother's calculations: it is destined to die by her hand. The moments of 'Stille' in this passage cover some of the most unspeakable actions in the play; bribery, abandoning of woman and child, and ultimately murder. Alfred only speaks to ask questions on matters of detail: his thoughts are a different matter.

'Bildungsjargon'

Just as music and silence play an essential part in unmasking what lies beneath the surface so too do the clichés and received ideas that pour out of the characters' mouths. In his *Gebrauchsanweisung* Horváth clearly indicated the way in which the dialogue should be spoken:

> Es darf kein Wort Dialekt gesprochen werden! Jedes Wort muß hochdeutsch gesprochen werden, allerdings so, wie jemand, der sonst nur Dialekt spricht und sich nun zwingt, hochdeutsch zu reden. Sehr wichtig! Denn es gibt schon jedem Wort dadurch die Synthese zwischen Realismus und Ironie. (*G.W. 8*, p. 663)

> Not a word of dialect is to be spoken! Every word must be spoken in correct German, though admittedly as if by people who normally only speak dialect and who are now straining themselves to speak correct German. This is very important! Since it is in this way that every word is imbued with the synthesis of realism and irony.

Elsewhere in the same text Horváth explains that what has replaced dialect is 'Bildungsjargon'—an acquired language or artificial jargon—and this is what must be spoken by his characters. Apart from the obvious use of foreign words and phrases, proverbs, quotations (and a misquotation from Goethe's poem *Selige Sehnsucht* when Oskar recites the last verse in part III scene 3) and clichés, the ideas and conversation are shot through with 'Bildungsjargon'. The Zauberkönig's speech at the engagement party is an excellent example of the form at its best:

Silentium, gleich bin ich fertig, und nun haben wir uns
hier versammelt, das heißt: ich hab euch alle eingeladen,
um einen wichtigen Abschnitt im Leben zweier blühen-
der Menschenkinder einfach, aber würdig, in einem
kleinen, aber auserwählten Kreise zu feiern. Es tut mir
nur heut in der Seele weh, daß Gott der Allmächtige es
meiner unvergeßlichen Gemahlin, der Mariann ihrem
lieben Mutterl selig, nicht vergönnt hat, diesen Freudentag ihres einzigen Kindes mitzuerleben. Ich weiß es aber
ganz genau, sie steht jetzt sicher hinter einem Stern dro-
ben in der Ewigkeit und schaut hier auf uns herab ... (Act
I, scene 3, *G.W. 1*, p. 179)

Just a minute, I shan't be much longer, and now we've all
gathered here, that's to say, I've invited you all here, to cele-
brate simply but with dignity, in a small but select circle, a very
important moment in the lives of these two, now in the flower of
their youth. My only deep regret today is that Almighty God has
not spared Marianne's dear precious mother, God rest her
soul, my unforgettable wife, to share this day of joy with her
only daughter. But I'm sure of one thing, she's somewhere up
there now in Heaven, standing behind a star and looking down
on us ...

From the first word here in Latin, through the polite pom-
posities and hypocrisies, Horváth shows mastery of the
speechmaker's jargon. The Zauberkönig says all the right
things, the formula is correct, and indeed he feels it his duty to
speak in such a way. What he thinks and does subsequently
show not only how 'unvergeßlich' his wife is (as he flirts with
Valerie and tells what he really thought of his wife) but also
how select the circle of friends is and how much this is a
'Freudentag' (for Marianne in particular as she throws the
engagement ring at Oskar's face). Seriousness and irony are
truly fused in this speech.

The meeting between Alfred and Marianne and their decla-
ration of love shows 'Bildungsjargon' in a less formalized
setting. From Alfred's first statement that he knew Marianne
would come out of the river at this place (how could he know

it?), the tone is fake and the emotions are cobbled together with borrowed phrases and spurious moral sentiments:

> ALFRED: Was haben wir aus unserer Natur gemacht? Eine Zwangsjacke. Keiner darf, wie er will.
> MARIANNE: Und keiner will, wie er darf.
> (*Stille*)
> ALFRED: Und keiner darf, wie er kann.
> MARIANNE: Und keiner kann, wie er soll—
> (*Alfred umarmt sie mit großer Gebärde, und sie wehrt sich mit keiner Faser—ein langer Kuß*) *Haucht*: Ich habs gewußt, ich habs gewußt—(Act I, scene 4, *G.W. 1*, p. 188)

> ALFRED: We've turned our real natures into a strait-jacket. Nobody's allowed to do what they want to do.
> MARIANNE: And nobody wants to do what they're allowed to do.
> (*Silence*)
> ALFRED: And nobody's allowed to do what they're able to do.
> MARIANNE: And nobody's able to do what they ought to do.
> (*Alfred embraces her dramatically and she makes no move to resist him. A long kiss.*)
> MARIANNE (*gets her breath*): I knew it, I knew it—

Once again the idea of some destiny is implied in Marianne's last words and, tragically, she at least really believes it when she takes the love-scene cliché one step further:

> Sie sollen uns finden—bleib mir, du, dich hat mir der Himmel gesandt, mein Schutzengel—(Act I, scene 4, *G.W. 1*, p. 190)

> I don't care if they find us. Stay with me, you've been sent down from Heaven, you're my guardian angel—

Marianne

Of all Horváth's female victims it is undoubtedly Marianne and Elisabeth (in *Glaube Liebe Hoffnung*) who most readily attract our sympathies. Although a victim of society and of her own feelings Marianne is no puppet: she has a strong but misguided will of her own. She is able to reject Oskar and her father with an intensity and passion that are admirable; her failing lies in not recognizing Alfred for what he is: a good-for-nothing whose idle philandering and spongeing have been evident from his first appearance—but not to Marianne. What makes her such a sympathetic character is not just the fact that she is used and broken by those around her, it is her obstinate refusal to accept Oskar, her loyalty to her child and, most important of all, her realization of the horror that surrounds her.

Marianne, daughter of the Zauberkönig, lives with him above the shop where they sell 'magic' and repair dolls. The only items that are seen to be sold, however, are toy soldiers, and wounded and dying ones at that. It has never been questioned by anyone (not even by Marianne) that she will marry the boy next door—who happens to be a butcher. Her father is despotic, treating Marianne as a surrogate wife since the death of her mother, and he even warns Oskar against treating her too gently:

> Ich glaub gar, daß du sie mir verwöhnst—also nur das nicht, lieber Oskar! Das rächt sich bitter! Was glaubst du, was ich auszustehen gehabt hab in meiner Ehe? Und warum? Nicht weil meine gnädige Frau Gemahlin ein bissiges Mistvieh war, sondern weil ich zu vornehm war, Gott hab sie selig! (Act I, scene 2, G.W. 1, pp. 172–3)

> I hope you're not spoiling her. Don't do that, Oskar, whatever you do. You'll suffer for it if you do. What do you think I had to put up with in my marriage? And why? Not because my lady wife was a bad-tempered old hag, God bless her, but because I could never bring myself to do anything dishonourable.

Oskar himself is always 'correct' in his treatment of Marianne but beneath the surface of all that he says and does, the butcher is ever present and his manifestations are sinister:

> Jetzt möcht ich in deinen Kopf hineinsehen können, ich möcht dir mal die Hirnschale herunter und nachkontrollieren, was du da drinnen denkst—(Act I, scene 2, G.W. 1, p. 172)

I wish I could see inside your head. I wish I could get inside your skull and find out what you're thinking in there—

and

Marianne. Ich hab dir mal gesagt, daß ich es dir nie wünsch, daß du das durchzumachen sollst, was du mir angetan hast—und trotzdem hat dir Gott Menschen gelassen—die dich trotzdem lieben—und jetzt, nachdem sich alles so eingerenkt hat,—Ich hab dir mal gesagt, Marianne, du wirst meiner Liebe nicht entgehn—(Act III, scene 4, *G.W. 1*, p. 251)

Marianne. I once told you I hoped you'd never have to go through what you made me suffer. And even now God has left you people who love you in spite of everything. And now everything's been put right like this ... I once told you, Marianne, you wouldn't escape my love ...

Apart from his words there are his kisses where he always inadvertently succeeds in hurting; his demonstration of ju-jitsu on Marianne; lastly there is the image of sticking the pig, an activity for which Oskar's appetite rises and falls, depending on how close he is to winning Marianne. Such is the man to whom she is engaged.

Her treatment at the hands of Alfred has already been touched on as has the loyalty she shows to her child. It is this child (to which she gives her father's name, Leopold, as a sign of love and respect) that is instrumental in bringing about her development as a character. From her dream of escape with Alfred she is reduced to the state of a mother who is desperate to look after her child, and it is this love which provides her with strength and a true sense of values. It is because of the child that she cannot confess in the Stephansdom:

Nein, das tu ich nicht,—Nein, davor hab ich direkt Angst, das ich es bereuen könnt.—Nein, ich bin sogar glücklich, daß ich es hab, sehr glücklich—(Act II, scene 7, *G.W. 1*, p. 216)

No, I'm not going to. No. I'd be frightened to think I could repent that. No, I'm happy I have him, very happy—

Here there is no arrogance, no illusion, and Marianne is still ready to turn to God as she does in humility and despair at the end of Act II.

> Wenn es einen lieben Gott gibt—was hast du mit mir vor, lieber Gott?—Lieber Gott, ich bin im achten Bezirk geboren und hab die Bürgerschul besucht, ich bin kein schlechter Mensch—hörst du mich?—was hast du mit mir vor, lieber Gott?—(*G.W. 1*, p. 217)

> If there is a God ... what's to become of me, God? Dear God I was born in Vienna 8 and I went to the local secondary school, I'm not a bad person ... are you listening? What's to become of me, God?

After all that she has to go through Marianne comes out with an integrity that allows her to speak with sincerity and full awareness of why she is agreeing to a reconciliation:

> Ich möcht jetzt nur noch was sagen. Es ist mir nämlich zu guter Letzt scheißwurscht—und das, was ich da tu, tu ich nur wegen dem kleinen Leopold, der doch nichts dafür kann—(Act II, scene 3, *G.W. 1*, p. 247)

> I just want to say one thing. When it really comes down to it, I don't give a shit. What I'm doing, I'm doing for Leopold, because none of this is his fault—

Alfred, Oskar, and her father, have all caused Marianne to suffer and as her degradation continues so she is stamped on harder by those around her. She loses her illusion of love, her aspirations to dance are twisted so that she becomes an artiste in a strip-club, she loses her baby at the hands of Alfred's sinister grandmother, she is arrested for theft and humiliated; worst of all the wheel turns full circle and she finds herself returned to Oskar, shop-soiled but none the less acceptable to him now that the baby is dead. Her despair is total as she makes one last defiant gesture:

> MARIANNE: Ich hab mal Gott gefragt, was er mit mir vorhat.—Er hat es mir aber nicht gesagt, sonst wär ich

nämlich nicht mehr da.—Er hat mir überhaupt nichts
gesagt.—Er hat mich überraschen wollen.—Pfui!
OSKAR: Marianne! Hadere nicht mit Gott!
MARIANNE: Pfui! Pfui! (*Sie spuckt aus*)
(*Stille*)
(Act III, scene 7, *G.W. 1*, p. 251)

> MARIANNE: I once asked God what was to become of me. He
> didn't tell me, otherwise I wouldn't be here any more. He
> didn't tell me anything. He wanted it to be a surprise. Damn
> Him!
> OSKAR: Marianne! Never quarrel with God!
> MARIANNE: Damn Him! Damn Him! (*She spits*)
> (*Silence*)

Repetition

To illustrate the infinity of stupidity Horváth gives this play
(and *Italienische Nacht*) a circular structure. Thus Valerie and
Alfred are reunited, Marianne and Oskar are reunited; the
play opens out in the Wachau and ends there, the evil frailty of
the grandmother dominating both scenes. The motif of death
is introduced in the first scene, both by Valerie who thinks of
tidying up her husband's grave (Alfred proposes to use his
winnings on the horses for this purpose), and also by the
grandmother who talks of her own death. In the final scene
it is the same characters who introduce the topic. The
grandmother, far from being moribund herself, is as if
rejuvenated by the act that she has committed and is at her
most horrific and most powerful as she dictates the letter
to Marianne telling her of little Leopold's death. Valerie,
who has shown human feeling for Marianne, now talks
again of graves (Alfred once more proposes to use his
winnings):

> Wir werden ihm einen schönen Grabstein setzen. Viel-
> leicht ein betendes Englein. (Act III, scene 7, *G.W. 1*, p.
> 250)

> We'll buy him a nice tombstone. A praying angel, something
> along those lines.

Although well-meant, Valerie's comment is about as inept as it could be, and the grandmother's letter the most callous and positively evil passage in the play.

With the exception of Marianne none of the characters have changed and they will all revert to their previous patterns of behaviour—Alfred to Valerie and the horses, Oskar to Marianne and the slaughter of pigs, the captain to his lottery results and the grandmother to her zither. The music too returns to the opening strains of *Tales from the Vienna Woods* ...

The 'Volksstück'

Although Horváth expressly stated that it was not his intention to revive an old form but rather to create a new one there are obvious points of comparison between the traditional 'Volksstück' and Horváth's 'Volksstücke', and it is useful to understand why he adopted this subtitle for most of his major plays (*Die Bergbahn, Italienische Nacht, Geschichten aus dem Wiener Wald, Kasimir und Karoline, Glaube Liebe Hoffnung*).

The home of the 'Volksstück' was Vienna in the eighteenth century and there were two main forms: the 'Zauberstück' (magic play) and the 'Lokalstück' (local play). The first descended from baroque drama and was set in a fairy-tale world through which a simple-minded tradesman trod his path; the second form was more satirical and was designed to make fun of contemporary trends and fashions. There was also a third title—the 'Besserungsstück' (morally improving play) which showed a character whose fault was cured by experiences in a dream (similar to the idea of Dickens's *A Christmas Carol*). All forms relied heavily on a musical element and the use of local settings and traditions. The only 'Volksstück' to achieve international reputation has been Schikaneder's libretto for the Mozart opera *Die Zauberflöte* (*The Magic Flute*).

The nineteenth century saw two important actor-writers

take up the 'Volksstück', and these were Raimund and Nestroy, both of whom Horváth much admired, in particular the
biting satire which Nestroy brought into the genre. By the end
of the century the form had fallen into disuse and it was not
until first Carl Zuckmayer and then Horváth revived it in the
nineteen-twenties that the term was used again in the theatre.
In a radio interview in 1932 Horváth was asked to explain
why he had chosen this category for his plays. He replied:

> Ich gebrauchte diese Bezeichnung 'Volksstück' nicht
> willkürlich, d.h. nicht einfach deshalb, weil meine Stücke
> mehr oder minder bayerisch oder österreichisch betonte
> Dialektstücke sind, sondern weil mir so etwas ähnliches,
> wie die Fortsetzung des alten Volksstückes vor-
> schwebte.—Des alten Volkstückes, das für uns junge
> Menschen mehr oder minder natürlich auch nur noch
> einen historischen Wert bedeutet, denn die Gestalten
> dieser Volksstücke, also die Träger der Handlung haben
> sich doch in den letzten zwei Jahrzehnten ganz unglaub-
> lich verändert.—... Es gibt eine ganze Anzahl ewig-
> menschlicher Probleme, über die unsere Großeltern
> geweint haben und über die wir heute lachen—oder
> umgekehrt ... Also: zu einem heutigen Volksstück gehö-
> ren heutige Menschen, und mit dieser Feststellung
> gelangt man zu einem interessanten Resultat: nämlich,
> will man als Autor wahrhaft gestalten, so muß man der
> völligen Zersetzung der Dialekte durch den Bildungsjar-
> gon Rechnung tragen. (*G.W. 1*, p. 11)

I did not use the category 'folk-play' arbitrarily, that's to say not
simply because my plays are marked by a dialect that is more or
less Bavarian or Austrian in its emphasis, but because I had in
mind something in the nature of a continuation of the old
folk-play. The old folk-play naturally is of little more than
historical interest for us young people, since the figures of these
plays, the protagonists, have changed out of all recognition in
the last two decades ... There is a whole range of recurrent
human problems which made our grandparents weep and which
make us laugh today—and vice versa ... To sum up: today's
folk-play requires today's people, and this brings one to an
interesting conclusion: if one wishes to portray faithfully as an

author one must take into account the fact that dialects have been totally decomposed by acquired jargon.

In the *Gebrauchsanweisung* Horváth reiterated much of what he had said in the interview but went even further in his attempt to define the category and the characters:

> Nun aber besteht Deutschland, wie alle übrigen europäischen Staaten zu neunzig Prozent aus vollendeten oder verhinderten Kleinbürgern, auf alle Fälle aus Kleinbürgern. Will ich also das Volk schildern, darf ich natürlich nicht nur die zehn Prozent schildern, sondern als treuer Chronist meiner Zeit, die große Masse. Das ganze Deutschland muß es sein! ... Mit vollem Bewußtsein zerstöre ich nun das alte Volksstück, formal und ethisch—und versuche die neue Form des Volksstückes zu finden. Dabei lehne ich mich mehr an die Tradition der Volkssänger an und Volkskomiker an, denn an die Autoren der klassischen Volksstücke. (*G.W. 8*, p. 662–3)

> Now in Germany as in all other European countries, ninety per cent of the people are either successful or frustrated petty bourgeois. And so if I want to portray the people, then obviously I won't portray the other ten per cent, but as a true chronicler of my time, the vast masses. It must be the whole of Germany!
> ... Quite deliberately I am destroying the old folk-play, both in its form and in its ethos—and I am attempting to find the new form of the folk-play. In doing so I turn more to the tradition of the folk-singers and folk-comedians than to the authors of the classical folk-plays.

The emphasis that Horváth intends is clear both in terms of character and milieu and there are also in *Geschichten aus dem Wiener Wald* elements of the traditional 'Volksstück' that are not so visible in his other 'Volksstücke'. The music and songs are associated almost exclusively with Vienna; Marianne's father is a 'Zauberkönig' (magic-king), albeit one who has lost his magic touch and certainly works no spells in this play! There is a traditional element in the grandmother figure although she is more of a witch than the benevolent, homely figure one would expect in the traditional play. Also there is an element of the 'Besserungsstück', since Marianne's 'dream-like' experiences with Alfred do lead her to self-awareness, even if this is a self-awareness from which no comfort is to be drawn. Lastly there is the 'happy ending'—a reunion that is a grotesque parody of its literary antecedents and a stark comment on 'real life'.

5

The Last 'Volksstücke'

Kasimir und Karoline

Like *Geschichten aus dem Wiener Wald*, this play has a setting
that arouses certain expectations: all of its 117 scenes are
acted out at the Munich 'Oktoberfest' against a background of
traditional music, circus entertainments, alcoholic revelry and
general merriment. The play's motto, 'Und die Liebe höret
nimmer auf' (And love never ends), has a bitter irony to it:
love here is a merry-go-round, a part of the entertainment and,
in contrast with the 'happy ending' of the previous play, partners are seen to be interchangeable and are not reunited at the
end. Relationships, like consumer goods, are expendable.
Once again, as in *Geschichten aus dem Wiener Wald*, the
Zeppelin appears, only this time it is no model but the real
thing. It hovers over the opening scene and is admired by all.
One of the dwarfs comments with a cliché that is particularly
ironic coming from his lips:

> Wenn man bedenkt, wie weit es wir Menschen schon
> gebracht haben—(scene 1, *G.W. 1*, p. 225)
>
> When you consider how far we human beings have developed
> . . .

The implications are sinister since the Zeppelin represents not
only the technological achievements but also the new political
force rising in Germany (even the tableau of the Zeppelin was
greeted with a spontaneous chorus of *Deutschland über alles* in
Geschichten aus dem Wiener Wald). The way in which it is
admired in this play, above all by freaks, is even more sinister,

in view of the way they were to be treated under Hitler's Third Reich.

The 'Oktoberfest' in Munich is still much as it was in Horváth's day and its uninhibited atmosphere is an ideal setting for unmasking the latent savagery and unconcealed stupidity of his characters.

The division of the play into two groups of fifty-five and sixty-one scenes respectively (the length of the two halves is in fact almost identical) is far less aleatory than it first appears. The very short scenes, some of which are no more than two words or a snatch of music, serve to give glimpses of changing relationships through fragments of conversation. It is as if characters were briefly glimpsed as they are whisked past on a carousel. These scenes and the action that takes place are more than a little reminiscent of Büchner's *Woyzeck*. The indoor scenes in the *Zuschauerraum, bei den Abnormitäten* (the tent where the freaks are on display) is very close to the *Schaubude* (show-booth) scenes in Büchner's play where the wonders of nature are displayed by a horse that can tell the time. It is here that Woyzeck's Marie is seduced by the Major, just as Karoline and Schürzinger (The word 'Schürze'—meaning apron—and 'Schürzenjäger'—ladies' man—giving an intimation of character here) begin to use the intimate 'du' and Karoline kisses Schürzinger.

In best theatrical style Horváth uses the interval in the freaks' show as the play's own interval; his spectators too are watching a freaks' show. But are their attitudes, their amorous affairs any more reputable than those of the characters on stage? It is the 'Abnormitäten' who are perhaps the only ones without moral deformities in this play. The intention of this break is obvious since the audience cannot fail to identify themselves with the spectators on stage, as both go to their interval.

Settings in *Glaube Liebe Hoffnung*

This last 'Volksstück', *Glaube Liebe Hoffnung* (*Faith, Charity, Hope*)*, subtitled '*Ein kleiner Totentanz in fünf Bildern*' (*A little dance of death in five pictures*), could hardly be more bleak in its choice of settings. The play is suffused with death from its outset and it marks the beginning of a blacker, altogether more tragic period in Horváth's writing. Act one opens with Elisabeth in front of an Anatomical Institute where bodies are laid out 'in Reih und Glied' (rank and file). She is attempting to sell her body for research after she is dead, so that she may have money on which to live now. The second act is set in the lingerie shop of Irene Prantl and here the specific stage direction is that the wax dummies are also

> in Reih und Glied, ähnlich wie die Körper im Anatomischen Institut
>
> in rank and file similar to the bodies in the Anatomical Institute.

Act three takes place in front of a Welfare Office, and an invalid comes limping out; like Elisabeth at the opening he has been refused assistance, although visibly disabled. The fourth act shows Elisabeth's 'möbliertes Zimmer' (furnished room), and despite Horváth's ironic (and impossible!) stage direction

> Das Ganze ist ein Bild des glücklichen Friedens zweier liebenden Herzen (*G.W. 1*, p. 359)
>
> The whole setting is the very picture of peaceful contentment between two loving hearts

there are white asters, graveyard flowers, on the table. In the final act, to the strains of Chopin's Funeral March, the policeman, Alfons Klostermeyer, is playing chess with a colleague at the police station. It is here that Elisabeth will be brought to die.

---

* Horváth has deliberately changed the biblical order *Glaube Hoffnung Liebe*, thus implying that the greatest of these is hope and *not* charity.

Demaskierung des Bewußtseins

This phrase, meaning 'the unmasking of man's consciousness', occurs several times in the *Gebrauchsanweisung* and is a theme that is central to Horváth's critical comments on the staging of his own plays. Since the *Gebrauchsanweisung* was written with *Kasimir und Karoline* in mind it is worth looking at this phrase in context and considering the author's sharp rejection of parody:

> Denn letzten Endes ist das Wesen der Synthese aus Ernst und Ironie die Demaskierung des Bewußtseins ...
> ... Aus all dem geht schon hervor, daß Parodie nicht mein Ziel sein kann—es wird mir oft Parodie vorgeworfen, das stimmt aber natürlich in keiner Weise. Ich hasse die Parodie! Satire und Karikatur—ab und zu ja. Aber die satirischen und karikaturistischen Stellen in meinen Stücken kann man an den fünf Fingern herzählen. Ich bin kein Satiriker, meine Herrschaften, ich habe kein anderes Ziel als wie dies: Demaskierung des Bewußtseins. (*G.W. 8*, p. 660)

> When it comes down to it the essence of this synthesis between seriousness and irony is the unmasking of man's consciousness ...
> ... It is apparent from all of this that parody cannot possibly be my aim—I am often accused of writing parody, but this is of course in no way true. I detest parody! Satire and caricature from time to time yes. But the passages of satire and caricature in my plays can be counted on the fingers of one hand—I am not a satirist, ladies and gentlemen, and I have no other aim than this: the unmasking of man's consciousness.

To illustrate this process at work it is best to consider one of the most obvious examples first. As the businessman Rauch (the name 'Smoke' connoting his hollow promises) and his friend from the law-court Speer ('Spear') smile and wave at the girls coming down the helter-skelter, they are really positioned there so that they can look up the girls' skirts, and this is indicated in the stage direction. But here the unmasking

is on both sides: the stage direction again clearly states that the
girls adjust their bras

> welche sich durch das Herabrutschen verschoben haben
> (*G.W. 1*, p. 271)

> which have slipped as they came down the slide.

Their clothing has, quite literally revealed things that were not
intended. In the same way their conversation, which cannot be
heard by the men, belies their smiling faces:

> (*Elli blickt ihn freudlich an—aber so, daß er es nicht hören
> kann*)
> Schnallentreiber dreckiger.
> (*Rauch grüßt geschmeichelt*)
> (*Wie zuvor*) Guten Abend, Herr Nachttopf!
> (*Rauch läuft das Wasser im Munde zusammen*)
> (*Wie zuvor*) Das tät dir so passen, altes Scheißhaus—
> Denk lieber an das Sterben als wie an das Gegenteil!
> (*Fröhlich ab mit Maria*). (scene 22, *G.W. 1*, p. 271)

> (*Elli gives him a friendly look—and then says, quietly enough for
> him not to hear*) Dirty pimp.
> (*Rauch is flattered and waves*)
> (*As above*) Good evening, Mr Chamber-pot!
> (*Rauch's mouth begins to water*)
> (*As above*) That'd just about suit you, you old shithouse—Why
> don't you think about dying rather than the opposite!
> (*Goes off cheerfully with Maria*)

Time and again unmasking is seen in the contrast between
what characters say behind one another's backs and when face
to face. After protesting his shyness and innocence to
Karoline, Schürzinger is totally unmasked and his real intentions are revealed in conversation with Rauch, who is his
employer. Although the scabrous intentions are thinly veiled
by the use of a historical anecdote, the two men understand
each other only too well; their thoughts are again apparent
beneath the two silences:

> RAUCH:—Hören Sie her: Ludwig der Fünfzehnte ging
> eines Abends mit seinem Leutnant und dessen Braut in

das Hippodrom. Und da hat sich jener Leutnant sehr
bald verabschiedet, weil er sich überaus geehrt gefühlt
hat, daß sein Monarch sich für seine Braut so irgendwie
interessiert.—Geehrt hat er sich gefühlt! Geehrt!
(*Stille*)
SCHÜRZINGER: Ja, diese Anekdote ist mir nicht unbe-
kannt. Jener Leutnant wurde dann bald Oberleut-
nant—
RAUCH: So? Das ist mir neu. (*Stille*)
SCHÜRZINGER: Darf ich mich empfehlen, Herr Kommer-
zienrat—(scene 80, *G.W. 1*, p. 303)

RAUCH:—Just listen: Louis the Fourteenth went to the hippo-
drome one evening with his lieutenant and the lieutenant's
bride. And there the lieutenant took his leave very smartly,
because he felt thoroughly honoured that his monarch should
take such an interest in his bride.—Honoured he felt!
Honoured!
(*Silence*)
SCHÜRZINGER: Yes, I'm not unaware of this anecdote. That same
lieutenant was then soon promoted—
RAUCH: Oh? That's new to me.
(*Silence*)
SCHÜRZINGER: May I be on my way now, sir—

Unemployment

While *Kasimir und Karoline* and *Glaube Liebe Hoffnung*
differ radically in their settings, they are thematically linked by
the way in which they illustrate the effects of unemployment.
Kasimir has just lost his job as a chauffeur and Elisabeth is out
of work because she had tried to pursue her job without having
the necessary permit. In each case the situation has a direct
effect on the stability of relationships.

Kasimir und Karoline

Kasimir's mood is one of gloom and self-pity from the first
scene. He has come to the *Oktoberfest* reluctantly and is
resentful of Karoline's security:

KASIMIR: ... du verdienst ja noch etwas und lebst bei
deinen Eltern, die wo pensionsberechtigt sind. Aber

ich habe keine Eltern mehr und steh allein in der Welt,
ganz und gar allein. (*G.W. 1*, p. 257)

> KASIMIR: ... you're still earning and you live with your parents
> and they're entitled to a pension. But I have no parents any
> more and stand alone in the world, utterly and completely
> alone.

Typically, Karoline is more loyal to her fiancé than he is to
her, in spite of the fact that she could probably have found a
partner with rather more social (and financial) standing than
Kasimir. Certainly this is her opinion. When she meets Schürzinger the conversation soon turns to unemployment and love:

> SCHÜRZINGER: Nehmen wir an, Sie lieben einen Mann.
>   Und nehmen wir weiter an, dieser Mann wird nun
>   arbeitslos. Dann läßt die Liebe nach, und zwar auto-
>   matisch.
> KAROLINE: Aber das glaub ich nicht!
> SCHÜRZINGER: Bestimmt!
> KAROLINE: Oh nein! Wenn es dem Mann schlecht geht,
>   dann hängt das wertvolle Weib nur noch intensiver an
>   ihm—könnt ich mir schon vorstellen.
> SCHÜRZINGER: Ich nicht. (*Stille*) (scene 4, *G.W. 1*, p. 258)

> SCHÜRZINGER: Let us suppose that you love a man. And let us
>   further suppose that this man now becomes unemployed.
>   Then love will decline and it will do so automatically.
> KAROLINE: But I don't believe that!
> SCHÜRZINGER: Definitely!
> KAROLINE: Oh no! If things are going badly then a woman of any
>   worth will stick to him even more solidly—that's what I
>   imagine.
> SCHÜRZINGER: Not me. (*Silence*)

In the silence that follows this exchange it is clear that the seed
sown by Schürzinger has not fallen on stony ground. Karoline
half gives herself away by asking him whether he can read
palms: this seemingly inconsequential question suggests that
Schürzinger has already begun to read her mind! Indeed it
does not take much to erode her feelings for Kasimir still
further and his own heartless treatment does nothing to

encourage her. As is almost always the case in relationships it is Kasimir—the man—whose behaviour is far more reprehensible than his fiancée's. Her pathetic attempts to return to him at the end of the play are greeted with disgust by Kasimir and with hypocritical scorn by Erna, her 'replacement':

> (*Karoline gibt ihm plötzlich einen Kuß*)
> KASIMIR: Zurück! Pfui Teufel! (*Er spuckt aus*) Brr!
> ERNA: Ich versteh das gar nicht, wie man als Frau so wenig Feingefühl haben kann. (scene 13, *G.W. 1*, p. 321)

> (*Karoline suddenly gives him a kiss*)
> KASIMIR: Get away! Damn you! (*he spits*) Ugh!
> ERNA: I don't understand how a woman can have so little sense of delicacy.

Certainly love declines—'die Liebe läßt nach'—but it is far more true of Kasimir than of Karoline. She had initially been drawn towards Schürzinger as 'ein gebildeter Mensch' (an educated person), who has charm, money and a job, yet it is she who is rejected by Kasimir, for all his sententious talk about lying:

> Hier dreht es sich doch nicht um deine Achterbahn, sondern um dein unqualifizierbares Benehmen, indem du mich angelogen hast! (scene 7, *G.W. 1*, p. 269)

> It is not a question of your rides on the roller-coaster but of your inexcusable conduct in lying to me.

While his unemployment may be seen as the starting point for the game of musical partners that takes place it is certainly no justification—for any of them.

Glaube Liebe Hoffnung

In his preface to this play, Horváth wrote that he had collaborated with a court reporter, Lukas Kristl, and the characters of Elisabeth and Alfons Klostermeyer are both based on people in a real court case. Elisabeth has been caught in a vicious circle: in order to work she needs a permit allowing her to

travel. Previously she had worked without one because she did
not have the necessary money to obtain it. Arrested by the
police and fined, she was eventually unable to keep up the
payments on the fine and so sent to prison for fourteen days.
On her release from prison she once again found herself in the
same hopeless position and so now tries to sell her body. One
of the employees at the Anatomical Institute takes an interest
in her because of the cudos attaching to her father's title (he
imagines that Inspektor refers to a customs inspector and not
to a mere insurance inspector!) and lends her the hundred and
fifty Marks. When her 'deceit' is brought to light she is once
again up before the courts. Elisabeth's plight is portrayed with
far more sympathy than that of Kasimir or Karoline. It really is
through no fault of her own that she is in this position, and her
attempts to find a way out, resorting to deceit, or rather to not
telling the full truth, are not to be seen as morally reprehensible—they are the desperate actions of a woman in an imp5oss-
ible situation. When the 'Sittenpolizei' (Vice Squad) burst into
her room and reveal the truth to Klostermeyer there is no
doubt whose side the spectator is bound to be on:

> SCHUPO: Du has mich belogen und das ist für mich der
> entscheidende Punkt.
> ELISABETH: Nein, deine Karriere, das ist er, dein
> entscheidender Punkt.
> SCHUPO: Nein! Aber zuerst kommt die Pflicht und dann
> kommt noch Ewigkeiten nichts! Radikal nichts!
> (*Stille*)
> ELIZABETH: Du Alfons. Zuvor—wie du da drinnen im
> Schrank warst, da habe ich dich beschützen wollen.
> (Act IV, scene 11, *G.W. 1*, p. 366)

> POLICEMAN: You have lied to me and that's the decisive factor.
> ELISABETH: No, your career, that's what it is, your decisive
> factor.
> POLICEMAN: No! But duty comes first and then for an eternity
> comes nothing! Absolutely nothing!
> ELISABETH: Alfons. Just now—when you were there in the cup-
> board I wanted to protect you.

It is after this that Elisabeth is completely broken; she has lost faith in herself and the world around her, hope for the future, and the love that she thought she had found (to give but one reading to the title of the play). In spite of what she has lost Elisabeth has one final outburst against Alfons:

> Glotz mich nicht so an! Geh mir aus den Augen, sonst reiß ich mir die Augen aus! Bild dir doch nicht ein, daß ich wegen dir ins Wasser bin, du mit deiner großen Zukunft! Ich bin doch nur ins Wasser, weil ich nichts mehr zum Fressen hab—wenn ich was zum Fressen gehabt hätt, meinst, ich hätt dich auch nur angespuckt?! Schau mich nicht so an!! (*Sie wirft mit der Schnapsflasche nach seinen Augen, verfehlt aber ihr Ziel.*) Da! (Act V, scene 14, *G.W. 1*, p. 377)

> Don't stare at me like that! Get out of my sight, otherwise I'll tear my eyes out! And don't imagine that I jumped in the water because of you, you with your great future! I only jumped in the water because I'd nothing left to eat—if I'd had anything to eat d'you think that I'd have so much as spat at you?! Don't stare at me like that!! (*She throws the Schnaps bottle at his face but misses.*) There!

When she dies a few moments later there is no appeal to God (indeed this play, moribund as it is, contains not even one appeal to an absent God) and her last 'delirious' words

> Da fliegen lauter so schwarze Würmer herum

> There are nothing but black worms flying around

not only conjure up the horror of the grave but also provide a fitting comment on the people who have surrounded her all through her life. It is left to Alfons, the 'tragic hero' of the play, to make one gesture of sympathy to her before returning to his own self-pity

> Ich hab kein Glück. Ich hab kein Glück.

> I have no luck. I never have any luck.

6

The Later Plays

Hin und her 1934

This play, written for a revolving stage, is set on a bridge crossing the river that forms the border between two countries. It is called a 'Posse' (farce) and deals comically with the plight of a stateless citizen, Havlicek. Its subject is not only pertinent to Horváth himself (who was at the time involved in renewing his Hungarian passport) but to all those displaced persons who grew in numbers before, during and after the war. The implications of this subject for a play are grim ones and one must remember Horváth's dictum that human life

> nur im einzelnen eine Komödie ist

> is only a comedy in individual episodes

In order to make the play comic Horváth not only shows the idiocies of beaucracy, he also makes Havlicek a resourceful character able to view his own fate with some humour, thus preventing the spectator from feeling too much pity for him. He carries messages between Konstantin (the border official on one side) and Eva (daughter of the official on the other bank and Konstantin's beloved) and is not above giving reprimands when he goes about it:

> Kommandieren laß ich mich aber nicht, Sie—wenn ich schon die Freundlichkeit hab, als ein wanderndes Billet-doux herumzulaufen. (*G.W. 3*, p. 221)

I won't let myself be given orders, you—when I'm kind enough
to run back and forth as a mobile billet doux.

Despite the revolve, the accompanying music and the comic
love affair, the play would be static were it not for the arrival of
other characters and the many humorous episodes that take
place. On the bridge is a 'Privatpädogog' (tutor) whose desul-
tory fishing is about as successful as Havlicek's attempts to
leave the bridge. The heads of state of the two countries have a
secret rendezvous on the bridge at night and Havlicek is
mistaken for his opposite number by the first statesman to
arrive. The ensuing dialogue shows Havlicek at his most
resourceful:

HAVLICEK (*beiseite*): Großer Gott! Ein Narr!
x: Es war eine selten glückliche Idee Ihrerseits, daß wir
uns hier auf dieser abgelegenen Grenzbrücke treffen,
hier können wir doch mal ausnahmsweise friedlich alle
Strittigkeiten, die unsere beiden Länder berühren,
berühren.
HAVLICEK: Interessant! (*beiseite*) Nur immer Recht
geben, sonst laüft er vielleicht noch Amok!
x: Wir leiden unter unseren Grenzen.
HAVLICEK: Oh wie wahr! (Scene 32, *G.W. 3*, p. 237)

HAVLICEK (*aside*): Good God! A lunatic!
x: It was an uncommonly happy idea on your part that we should
meet on this remote border bridge; here we can, in this one
exceptional case, touch on all those areas of dispute which
touch our respective countries, in peace.
HAVLICEK: Interesting! (*aside*) Always agree with him, other-
wise he still might run amok!
x: We suffer from our borders.
HAVLICEK: Oh how true!

and a few lines later:

x: Oh, wir verstehen uns bereits, lieber Freund—darf ich
Sie 'Freund' nennen? Sie stehen so herrlich über diesen
Dingen!
HAVLICEK: Ich steh nur zwischen zwei Grenzen. (*G.W. 3*,
p. 238)

> x: Oh, we understand each other already, dear friend—may I
> call you 'friend'? You stand so splendidly aloof from these
> things!
> HAVLICEK: I am only standing between two borders.

Havlicek imagines X to be a madman and easily slips into his
'humouring' role. It is a classic comic situation of mistaken
identity, and the effect of Havlicek's two comments on his own
situation is comic rather than tragic. Indeed the play, with
its happy ending, is light-weight, and it is only in looking carefully at the primitive chauvinism and zeal of the two border
guards (and of course Havlicek's hapless position) that one
discerns the existence of a heartless and sinister bureaucracy
at work.

Himmelwärts 1934–5

Horváth called this play a 'Märchen' (fairy tale) and it certainly has more than a few similarities with the settings and
characters of its literary antecedents—Raimund, Nestroy and
Grillparzer all come to mind. In Horváth's case the move away
from the social and political material that had marked his
earlier plays is not difficult to understand. In these uneasy
early days of Nazism Horváth had to tread carefully, creating a
work that would appear politically neutral, while offering the
public an acceptable and familiar popular entertainment. He
had already written a short undated play fragment called
Himmelwärts. In this fairy tale from the technological age an
astronaut by the name of Kasimir is launched into space to the
cheers of the jubilant masses. The opening scene, immediately
before the launching, contains speeches both from the presi-
dent of what is clearly a strongly authoritarian régime and also
by the constructor of the rocket—both sing the praises of the
New Society and its technological miracles. But the Heaven
into which Kasimir finds himself propelled is more reminiscent
of the Kitsch image of Vienna suggested in *Geschichten aus
dem Wiener Wald*: there is wine, food and music, indeed only

women are absent, and Kasimir is able to dispense with them, given all his other creature comforts!

There is no rocket launched into heaven in the 1934 play but it too has music and Kitsch elements rather than mystical ones:

> Hoch über den höchsten Wolken hängt der Himmel voller Geigen. Vor dem geschlossenen Himmelstor hängt ein lustiger Briefkasten. (*G.W. 3*, p. 275)

> High up above the highest clouds Heaven is hung with violins. Outside the closed Pearly Gates there is a cheery letter-box.

Newspapers are delivered here too and Saint Peter comments dispassionately (but there are ominous overtones here and in other places in the play):

> Schauns gestern zum Beispiel habens auf der Erde drunten wieder einmal eine Masse Leute unschuldig hingerichtet—lauter Fehlurteile und trotzdem kommens all miteinander in die Höll! (*G.W. 3*, p. 299)

> Look at yesterday for example: down there on earth they executed another lot of innocent people—the whole lot misjudgements and they'll all go to Hell together just the same!

At the bottom of the three-level stage Hell is reminiscent of a badly organized torture chamber, run by incompetent bureaucratic clowns rather than traditional 'devils'. The Devil himself recalls with nostalgia the balmy days when he too was in Heaven. There is a good deal of friendly banter between him and his junior devils (who always address him as 'Euer Ungnaden'—Your Ungrace); puns on 'der Teufel soll ihn holen' (the devil take him) and 'diese Schlamperei schreit zum Himmel' (approximating to 'This sloppiness is enough to make a saint swear') abound, but the language is more that of slapstick than of terror.

Between this Kitsch Heaven and the fire and brimstone comedy team down below, the main action of the play—on earth—bears more resemblance to that of the earlier plays. It is centred around the sad and neglected Luise Steinthaler, whose progress is watched over anxiously by her mother in Heaven and, in anticipation of winning her immortal soul, by the Devil below. Like Marianne (and perhaps incidentally like Maria Elsner, to whom Horváth was briefly married, 1933–4) Luise has artistic aspirations; unlike Marianne she is able to realize these ambitions and to become a famous opera singer. This is brought about, after weeks of waiting, by means of a contract with the Devil. Perhaps it is not too fanciful to see in this a parallel with the artist in Hitler's Germany—selling her soul in order to be an artistic success. At the end of the play however the Devil relents, her contract with him is torn up, she loses her singing voice and becomes once more a simple girl with the prospect of a marriage that will bring if not happiness then at least contentment. This marriage is to a certain Lauterbach who, having served his term in Hell but not yet being good enough for Heaven, illustrates the play's theme—reconciliation to the simple pleasures of life. This theme of reconciliation is even extended to the Devil in the final scene: he has shown humanity in releasing Luise from her contract and may even have the chance of making good, as Saint Peter says:

> Wenn du alle deine Kontrakte so löst, wie jenen, dann nimmer lang. (*G.W. 3*, p. 324)

> If you dissolve all your contracts as you've done this one then it won't be long.

Figaro läßt sich scheiden 1936

Although completed in 1936 (the same year as his Don Juan) Horváth had made sketches for his play some time before, and the title was originally to have been *Figaro der Zweite* (*Figaro the Second*). Instead Horváth chose a title that is a reversal of the traditional situation, a technique that has already been seen in his treatment of the 'Volksstück'. The play spans several years, a much longer period than any other Horváth play, and shows the time from Figaro's fight with his master, Count Almaviva, up to the moment when the true revolution breaks out.

Horváth's preface to the play is once again important since it gives a clear idea of his intentions:

> Die Komödie *Figaro läßt sich scheiden* beginnt einige Jahre nach Beaumarchais' *Hochzeit des Figaro*. Trotzdem habe ich es mir erlaubt, das Stück in unserer Zeit spielen zu lassen, denn die Probleme der Revolution und Emigration sind erstens: zeitlos, und zweitens: in unserer Zeit besonders aktuell. Unter der in dieser Komödie stattfindenden Revolution ist nicht also die große Französische von 1789 gemeint, sondern schlicht nur eine jegliche Revolution, denn jeder gewaltsame Umsturz läßt in seinem Verhältnis zu dem Begriff, den wir als Menschlichkeit achten und mißachten, auf den gleichen Nenner bringen. In der *Hochzeit des Figaro* wetterleuchtet die nahe Revolution, in *Figaro läßt sich scheiden* wird zwar voraussichtlich nichts wetterleuchten, denn die Menschlichkeit wird von keinen Gewittern begleitet, sie ist nur ein schwaches Licht in der Finsternis. Wollen wir immerhin hoffen, daß kein noch so großer Sturm es erlöschen kann. (*G.W. 4*, p. 653)

> The comedy *Figaro gets a divorce* begins some years after Beaumarchais' *The Marriage of Figaro*. Nevertheless I have taken the liberty of setting the play in our own time because the problems of revolution are firstly: timeless, and secondly: especially topical in our time. It is not the great French Revolution of 1789 that is meant here but quite simply any revolution, since every powerful upheaval has the same common denominator in its relationship to that which we respect, or disdain, as humanity. In *The Marriage of Figaro* there are rumbles of the coming revolution; in *Figaro gets a Divorce* there will probably be no rumbles, for humanity is not accompanied by any storms, it is only a weak light in the darkness. Let us hope all the same that no storm, however great, will be able to extinguish it.

The play opens in total darkness and the penultimate scene in the last act repeats the same dialogue, although the roles are redistributed as relationships have changed in the play. More

significant and altogether more optimistic is the final scene, set
in the former country seat of Count Almaviva, where Figaro
and Susanne are reunited.

As he had done in *Hin und her* here too Horváth does not
make the homelessness of his characters a real cause for
concern: they are well able to cope and it is not long before
Figaro is managing the most prosperous barber's shop in
Großhadersdorf! Susanne is a far more lovable character than
her husband (and yet he too is not without a rascally charm)
and her experiences are similar to those of Marianne. Figaro
refuses to give her a child, she has an affair with another and is
abandoned by Figaro, while she continues to love him. Figaro
is however no Oskar, and there is always communication
between the two, and love. Figaro's faults lie in his readiness to
abandon his principles, to adapt himself too readily to new
circumstances—in short he is an opportunist. As Susanne says
to him in act II:

> Mein Figaro war der erste, der selbst einem Grafen
> Almaviva auf der Höhe seiner Macht die Wahrheit ins
> Gesicht sagte, du wahrst die Form in Großhadersdorf!
> Du bist ein Spießer, er war ein Weltbürger! Er war ein
> Mann, und du! (Act II, scene 2, *G.W. 4*, p. 432)

> My Figaro was the first person to say the truth, even to a Count
> Almaviva at the height of his power, you just play at keeping up
> appearances here in Großhadersdorf! You are a narrow-
> minded bourgeois, he was a citizen of the world! He was a man
> and you!

In Horváth's vocabulary a Spießer is the most despicable, as
well as the commonest form of human being (see his definition
of the Spießer in the opening of the eponymous novel (*G.W. 5*,
p. 147)). The difference is that Figaro is lucid, critical and full
of life; it is true that his 'Spießer' elements make him a less
amiable figure than Beaumarchais' hero* but he is redeemed

---

* It is interesting to note how close Horváth was to the Beaumarchais'
original in this example: 'Was tat er denn, der Herr Graf, um so viele Vorzüge
zu verdienen? Er gab sich die Mühe auf die Welt zu kommen, und das war die

by his intelligence, his cheeky wit, and not least by his inability to stop loving and needing Susanne.

Der jüngste Tag 1936–7

In this play the problem of guilt and retribution is dealt with more overtly than in any other work by Horváth (with the possible exception of the novel *Jugend ohne Gott*). The economic background plays no vital role: the main protagonists are neither unemployed nor do they lose their jobs; the entire play involves the build-up of guilt as the tissue of lies and deceit becomes more involved. The spark for all of this is one brief kiss that Anna gives Hudetz and not even a passionate kiss at that, since it is designed only to arouse the jealousy of Hudetz's wife:

> (*Sie [Anna] lächelt boshaft, küßt ihn plötzlich und deutet nach dem ersten Stock.*) Jetzt hat sies gesehen, daß ich Sie geküßt hab, was? (*Sie lacht*) Jetzt gibts aber dann was? (*Sie lacht*). (Bild I, *G.W. 2*, p. 541)
>
> (*She [Anna] smiles maliciously, kisses him suddenly and points to the first floor*) Now she's seen that I've kissed you, eh? (*She laughs*) Now there'll be trouble, won't there? (*She laughs*)

It is only seconds later that the express train hurtles past and Hudetz has forgotten to give the signal. Eighteen people are killed and countless others wounded. Now Hudetz, ever the 'pflichttreuer Beamter' (dutiful official), depends on Anna's silence, and with her statement that he gave the signal on time, and her father's attack on Hudetz's wife, sympathy for the hen-pecked Hudetz grows, although the spectator knows that Frau Hudetz is right:

---

einzige Arbeit seines ganzen Lebens . . .' (*G.W. 4*, p. 445) (What did he do, the count, to earn so many advantages? He gave himself the bother of being born and that was the only work of his whole life . . .'), and: 'Qu'avez-vous fait pour tant de biens? Vous vous êtes donné la peine de naître, et rien de plus . . .' (*Le Mariage de Figaro*, Act V, scene 3).

Ich sage die Wahrheit und werde alles beschwören! Sie hat ihm einen Kuß gegeben, nur um mich zu ärgern, aber es gibt einen Gott der Rache und drum hat er das Signal versäumt—ich kanns beschwören, beschwören, beschwören—(Bild II, *G.W. 2*, p. 551–2)

I'm telling the truth and will swear to everything! She gave him a kiss, only to annoy me, but there is a God of vengeance and that's why he missed the signal—I can swear to it, swear to it, swear to it—

This is the second time in the play that divine intervention has been mentioned and it is an idea that receives even fuller treatment in *Jugend ohne Gott*, in a court scene that owes much to the one in this play.

After the disculpation of Hudetz it is Anna who is troubled by her conscience, and in the central scene of the play, when she meets Hudetz some months after the disaster (appropriately their rendez-vous takes place beneath the pillars of the railway viaduct at night), she reveals how she is haunted by the dead:

Ich hör noch immer das Geschrei—ich darf nicht allein sein, Herr Vorstand, dann kommen die Toten, sie sind bös auf mich und wollen mich holen—(Bild IV, *G.W. 2*, p. 566)

I can still hear the screams—I can't be alone, stationmaster, the dead come to me then, they're angry with me and want to take me—

Anna's remorse is so great that it becomes a threat to Hudetz and he is now incapable of repentance and forced to murder Anna. When the play reaches its climax it is once again night and the action moves into the surreal: the ghosts of the dead appear to Hudetz, but not in a dream since they are present before Hudetz arrives. These characters, who now include Anna in their number, are living with the truth. As Anna says

Ich kann nicht mehr lügen (Bild VII, *G.W. 2*, p. 586)

I can't lie any more.

As always in Horváth's heaven the beer is free but the truth must be paid for and lived with; no more masks are possible. For Hudetz it means the acceptance of a higher judgement than any human one:

> Die Hauptsach ist, daß man sich nicht selber verurteilt oder freispricht—(Bild VII, *G.W. 2*, p. 588)

> The main thing is that it is not for us to condemn or to acquit ourselves—

Don Juan kommt aus dem Krieg 1936

Although *Himmelwärts* is a play that appears to deal directly with the problems of life, death and the hereafter, it is a remarkably un-supernatural work—devils and angels alike are rather familiar and almost homely figures, while the problems of guilt and retribution are dealt with in a light-hearted manner. It is in *Don Juan* and *Der jüngste Tag* that one has far more sense of the beyond, and the preoccupations of both the author and his characters are very much with guilt and the possibility of redemption in an after-life.

Once again Horváth goes back to a well-tried literary theme in *Don Juan*, even recalling Mozart's *Don Giovanni* in the scene at the opera. But his Don Juan, unlike Mozart's or Molière's, is already a broken man at the beginning of the play. Indeed he bears more resemblance to Brecht's returning soldier, Andreas Kragler (in *Trommeln in der Nacht*), since both men return home from the war to search for their respective fiancées. The play is set shortly after the end of World War I, and Don Juan returns with a heart that has been seriously weakened by the effects of pneumonia. The stage directions indicate that he is constantly clutching at his heart. Several times he refers to this weakness, the physical manifestation of a spiritual state. Horváth's Don Juan, unlike his literary predecessors, is portrayed with extreme sympathy, and it is he who is the victim. He is also a repentant man; the war has made him want to be loyal to his bride, however much he may have deceived her in the years gone by. Unfortunately for him he cannot escape his past character so easily, and his haunting, moribund charm bewitches all the women he encounters, from ageing widows to schoolgirls. In his preface Horváth wrote:

> Er ist der große Verführer, der immer und immer von den Frauen verführt wird. (*G.W. 2*, p. 591)

> He is the great seducer who is again and again seduced by women.

Don Juan is the only male character in the play, and the thirty-five female roles are to be played by nine actresses since

> ...es gibt nämlich keine fünfunddreißigerlei Frauen, sondern bedeutend weniger.

> There are not in fact thirty-five different types of women but significantly fewer.

The play is very short, and Horváth instructed that its three acts should be performed without a break; the settings should only be suggested, and it is the dialogue which should carry the weight of the play.

By setting the play in the immediate aftermath of war (in the opening scene firing is still going on and Don Juan makes his appearance in uniform) Horváth is able to illustrate social and economic changes, their effect on individuals and more particularly on the role of women. At the same time Don Juan, with his legendary power over women, shows how some aspects of human nature will never change, regardless of circumstances.

The war has decimated the male population and women have begun to take over in professions that had once been male preserves. Women have had to become self-sufficient, and the lesbian fashion designers show how men have, apparently, become superfluous to some: they even call each other Peter and Charlie! This is no cry for liberation on Horváth's part and the way in which Peter/Alice falls for Don Juan explodes the myth of self-sufficiency. In the same way his landlady's elder daughter, for all her crypto-Marxist patter—

> Die Beziehung zwischen den Geschlechtern ist für uns überhaupt kein Problem mehr, ist ja nur eine Funktion, wie Essen und Trinken! (Act III, *G.W. 2*, p. 635)
>
> The relationship between the sexes is not a problem for us any more, it's just a function, like eating and drinking!

—is drawn to Don Juan and reduced to tears when he tells her that he finds her offensive. Women have assumed roles that are not natural to them. Horváth, who certainly appears to have shared some of his hero's magnetism, shows these changes as no more than superficial ones, brought about by necessity. His tenderness and sympathy for the plight of women is abundantly clear in many of his plays, but it is their vulnerability and femininity, rather than their liberation and social rights, that he seeks to protect.

Don Juan, once he is established as a kind of art dealer, describes himself as a hyena of the inflation. This inflation has eroded salaries, pensions and savings, and the bill in a café amounts to three million marks—to no one's surprise. In this economic turmoil people will buy anything that is likely to retain its value, and works of art were then, as now, one of the surest hedges against inflation. In this 'career' too it seems as though Don Juan is successful almost because women seek to buy a part of him when they buy from him. This is best exemplified by the lady who declares that the Daumier she had bought from him is a fake. The whole conversation is loaded with sexual and emotional innuendo from the opening sentence, and the Daumier is as much a metaphor for feelings as a real painting. Don Juan offers to return the lady's cheque and then drops it over the balcony with the words

> Jetzt ist er drunten. Adieu. Man hält ihn für nichts. (Act II, *G.W. 2*, p. 623)
>
> It's down there now. Goodbye. Now it's worthless.

He might equally be referring to her emotions: it is not only in money that inflation is rampant.

Don Juan himself is searching not so much for a person to love as for perfection,

> also etwas, was es auf Erden nicht gibt (*G.W. 2*, p. 592)

in order words, something which does not exist on earth.

His search brings him to find one feature in each woman that reminds him of someone:

> Ihr Lächeln erinnerte mich an eine Frau ... (Act I, *G.W. 2*, p. 596)

Your smile reminded me of a woman ...

but the fiancée he is searching for has been dead a long time. He goes on searching throughout the play, increasingly hounded by the women he meets, until at last he arrives at his fiancée's former home. He sees two children smashing a snowman to pieces and asks them what it has done to hurt them. In the final scene he, too, becomes a snowman (as does the soldier in the novel *Ein Kind unserer Zeit*), which marks the end of his search: a frozen death and the prospect of the fires of Hell:

> es wird immer wärmer—Adieu, Schneemann—(*G.W. 2*, p. 646)

it's getting warmer all the time—Goodbye, snowman—

Pompeji 1937

The idea of 'unmasking' characters has been seen often enough in Horváth's earlier plays, and it is as if in his last work for the stage he had wanted to show the device in its most literal form. *Pompeji* is a reworking of the three act play *Ein Sklavenball*, omitting the singing and dancing of the earlier play and having a slightly less flippant mood.* It is set 'im Altertum' (in antiquity), and the language is decidedly and deliberately anachronistic, ranging from K. R. Thago's (the initials and name being a word-play on the German name for Carthage) Yiddish tone to the twentieth century commonplaces uttered by the Praetor. The persecution of the slaves and the violent racial hatred also have sinister overtones in the context of Germany between the wars. Despite the settings in all his later plays Horváth never loses sight of the contemporary situation and the seemingly innocuous parallels have an uncomfortable ring to them.

The play opens with a tableau:

> Alle Personen tragen pompejanischen Masken, die die wesentlichen Züge ihrer Charaktere, so wie man sich selbe eben landläufig vorstellt, darstellen sollen. (*G.W. 4*, p. 593)

> All the characters wear Pompeiian masks, which should illustrate the essentials of their personalities just as one would expect them to be.

One by one the masks are removed to reveal characters very different from those suggested by the painted features: the haetera Lemniselenis is not a cheeky little tart but

> ein schönes Kind mit traurigen Augen und einem frühverbitterten Zug

*Gone for instance is the amusing but somewhat gratuitous Goethe parody: Glaube den Reichen/Sie haben Recht/Das Armselige/Wird immer vertan/ Das Ewig-Geldliche/Zieht uns hinan! (*G.W. 4*, p. 548) (Believe the rich/ They are right!/ What is poor/ Is always squandered/ The eternal-financial/ Draws us onwards). C.f. End of *Faust II*: CHORUS MYSTERICUS: Das Unbeschreibliche/ Hier ist's getan/ Das Ewig-Weibliche/ Zieht uns hinan. (The ineffable/ Here is performed/ The eternal-feminine/ Draws us onwards.)

A more significant change is that K. R. Thago, far from disappearing beneath the waves as he does in *Ein Sklavenball*, himself becomes a convert to Christianity. Such a change really strengthens the hypothesis that Horváth wanted his point to be unmistakable, as does the appearance of the man who writes letters to whole towns (i.e. Saint Paul) in the final scene.

a beautiful child with sad eyes and a prematurely embittered expression

Matrosa is not an old Madam but

eine brave alte Frau

a worthy old lady

Praegnium is not a sharp little rascal but has

ein mageres trotziges Gesicht

a thin defiant face

The discrepancy between the acquired social role and the real person beneath is made quite explicit: even the overseer of the slaves removes his cruel, mean mask to reveal

ein rundes, gutmütiges Gesicht

a round, good-humoured face

In case the audience has missed the point one of the senior slaves, Toxilus, comments:

Komisch, daß ich dein Gesicht noch nie gesehen hab—hm. Nein, roh und niederträchtig sieht es nicht aus, eher ein bisserl blöd—(Bild I, *G.W.4,* p. 595)

Funny, I've never seen your face before—hm; no, it doesn't look cruel and mean, it looks a bit stupid more than anything—

The action of this 'Komödie eines Erdbebens' (comedy of an earthquake) takes place at the foot of the rumbling volcano, Vesuvius, that is to erupt at the end of the play. Lemniselenis escapes from her master, K. R. Thago, and the story shows her attempts to get the six hundred pieces of silver needed to buy her freedom. This inevitably recalls Elisabeth's situation in *Glaube Liebe Hoffnung,* and is only one of many elements borrowed from earlier plays. She, however, like her brother, the coiner Bagnio, is well able to handle both her problems and her relationships, and the tone is light-hearted throughout. Once again God ('der neue Gott' of Christianity rather than the Old Testament God) becomes a leitmotif in the play, first mentioned almost casually by Matrosa, subsequently gaining in importance, as Thago himself becomes associated with the Christians. Lemniselenis in Bild V seizes the problem of guilt, as she asks to be punished with Toxilus and refuses to go on lying. She has developed a strong sense of this aspect of Christianity when she says:

Kein Mensch ist unschuldig (*G.W. 4*, p. 634)

No human being is without guilt

and the Praetor realizes that this is a Christian sentiment:

Dafür lassen sich Leute im Zirkus zerreißen (*G.W. 4*, p. 635)

People are torn apart in the arena for that sort of thing.

Lastly, the play's final words are from the mouth of 'der Herr' (Saint Paul) in the catacombs:

Redet doch nicht so viel, Gott hört auch, wenn ihr schweigt (*G.W. 4*, p. 645)

Just don't talk so much, God hears you, even if you are silent.

This contrasts sharply with the Praetor's appeal to 'the Gods' (reminiscent of Marianne's appeal to God in *Geschichten aus dem Wiener Wald*), an appeal that is immediately followed by the eruption of Vesuvius:

Oh Jupiter, allmächtiger, hehrer Sohn der Rhea, höchster Gott, aus dessen Händen Reichtum, Hoffnung, Heil entströmt—warum erschlägst Du das Recht mit Deinem Blitz und läßt das Unrecht triumphieren? Sagt, Götter, was habt Ihr vor mit meiner Welt?! (*G.W. 4* p. 644)

Oh Jupiter, almighty, sublime son of Rhea, highest God, out of whose hands flow wealth, hope and salvation—why do You strike what is just with Your lightning and allow what is unjust to triumph? Tell me, Gods, what do You intend to do with my world?!

7

From Plays to Novels

Although it was not until 1937 that Horváth devoted himself exclusively to the writing of novels he had, throughout his literary career, produced a number of prose works and fragments, many of which remained unpublished during his lifetime. The earliest had been the *Sportmärchen* of 1923–4 which were published in various newspapers and magazines. They are witty, epigrammatic pieces, many of which take the form of a dialogue between two personified abstracts, e.g. *Start und Ziel* (*Start and Finish*) or objects, e.g. *Der große und der kleine Berg* (*The large mountain and the small mountain*). *Was ist das?* (*What is that?*) gives an example of the succinct style and pointed wit:

> Zwei Schwergewichte werden als Zwillinge geboren und hassen sich schon in der ersten Runde ihres Daseins. Aber nie reicht die Kraft, um den anderen im freien Stil zu erwürgen, nie wirken die heimlich im Ring verabreichten Gifte genügend gefährlich und alle Schüsse aus dem Hinterhalt prallen von den zu Stein trainierten Muskelteilen (vom Gürtel aufwärts!) ab.
>
> Und so leben die beiden neunzig Lenze lang.
>
> Aber eines Nachts schläft der eine beim offengelassenen Fenster, hustet dann morgens und stirbt noch am selbigen Abend.
>
> Was ist das?
>
> Ein Punktsieg. (*G.W. 5,* p. 39)

Two heavy weights are born twins and hate each other from the very first round of their existence. Neither one has the strength to strangle the other in open combat, nor do any of the poisons

that are secretly passed into the ring work effectively and all the
shots fired from ambushes bounce off the muscles that have
become rock-hard (from the belt upwards!)
    And so they both live for ninety years.
    But one night one of them sleeps by an open window, starts
coughing in the morning and dies the very same evening.
    What is that?
    A win on points.

Death is a recurrent theme in these mini-dramas (in *Was ist
das?* one recognizes a motif that comes up in *Geschichten aus
dem Wiener Wald*) and there are sinister undertones in many
of them. The other twenty or so short stories and fragments
that are to be found in the collected works are more of interest
for the themes and episodes that are also found, in modified
form, in the plays. Almost all deal with the 'Kleinbürgertum'
(petite bourgeoisie) and their characters include waiters, wait-
resses, grandmothers, and a range of petty officials. *Charlotte –
Roman einer Kellnerin* (*Charlotte—Novel of a Waitress*) contains one of Horváth's most bitter statements on God and is
important because of its place in any treatment of the theme of
God in Horváth's work:

> Gott sprach: Mein Gott, jetzt erfinden sie sogar
> Serums, wie soll das enden? Jetzt gibt es schon keine
> Cholera mehr, keine Pest in zivilisierten Gegenden.
> Nur gut, daß sie die Syphilis noch nicht ganz heilen
> können.
>   Und er bestimmte den Erzbischof von Prag, der
> sprach: Man darf nicht gegen die Krankheiten kämpfen,
> sie sind Gottes Prüfungen. Wenn einer Geschwüre hat
> und Knochenfraß so helft ihm nicht, denn warum hat er
> sich mit dem Fräulein Kitty Mesalka abgegeben? Wie? –
> Aber die Welt wurde immer ungläubiger und Gottes
> Stimme drang nicht in die Laboratorien. Sie machte Halt
> vor der Klinik.
>   Später kam Gott auf eine sehr gute Ausrede. Er sagte,
> er hätte es sich überlegt. Die Dyphtherie sei ab heute eine
> Harmlosigkeit. Aber die Menschen sollen nur nicht zu
> frech werden, denn zum Beispiel Zuckerkranke sind
> immer noch unheilbar.

Gott ersann immer neue Bazillen. Seine Erfindungs-
gabe ist göttlich. Aber der Mensch wehrte sich: je nach
Geldbörse.
Und Gott sprach: Es werde Krieg!
Und es ward Krieg. Und Gott sah, daß es gut war.
(*G.W. 8*, p. 412–13)

And God said: My God, now they're even inventing serums,
where's it going to end? There's no cholera any longer and no
more plagues in civilized countries. It's a good thing that they
can't yet cure syphilis effectively.

And he gave a command to the Archbishop of Prague who
spoke as follows: One should not fight against illness, they are
God's trials. If a man howls let him howl. If a man has abscesses
and gangrene then don't help him—why did he get involved
with Miss Kitty Mesalka, eh? But the world became increasingly
unbelieving and God's voice did not penetrate into the
laboratories, it stopped in front of the hospital.

Later God hit on a very good way out. He said He'd thought
the matter over. Diphtheria would be harmless as of that day.
But people should not become too cocksure since diabetics for
example were still incurable.

God thought up more and more new bacilli. His power of
invention is simply divine. But man defended himself: each one
according to his purse.

And God said: Let there be war!
And there was war. And God saw that it was good.

The only full-length novel that Horváth saw published in
Germany was *Der ewige Spießer* (*The Eternal Petit
Bourgeois*).* It is made up of a series of loosely connected
episodes that occur on a journey to the World Exhibition in

---

* Because of its definition of the 'Spießer' (the type of character Horváth
most wanted to unmask) his prefatory note is worth quoting:

'Der Spießer ist bekanntlich ein hypochondrischer Egoist, und so trachtet er
danach, sich überall feige anzupassen und jede neue Formulierung der Idee zu
verfälschen, indem er sie sich aneignet ...
... Der Verfasser wagt natürlich nicht zu hoffen, daß er durch diese Seiten ein
gesetzmäßiges Weltgeschehen beeinflussen könnte, jedoch immerhin! (The
petit bourgeois is, as everybody knows, an egoist with hypochondria, and so
he strives to adapt himself to everything in a cowardly way and to falsify every
newly formulated idea by appropriating it for himself ...
... The author naturally doesn't dare to hope that these pages might influence
an inevitable world event, but nonetheless ...).

Barcelona (a trip that the author himself had made in 1929). Once again one finds many incidents and character types which are also to be seen in the stage works, in both those written before and those written after the novel was published. One point of interest is the way in which the thoughts (so often covered by moments marked 'Stille' in the plays) are here given expression. While holding an apparently 'polite' conversation in a railway carriage, Schmitz's thoughts reveal what is left unsaid:

> Und Schmitz dachte: Vielleicht war es sogar blöd von mir, daß ich mich dem gleich angeboten habe als Reisebegleiter. Sicher war es blöd. Oh, wie bin ich blöd! Und warum bin ich blöd? Weil ich ein weicher Mensch bin ... (*G.W. 5*, p. 196.)

> And Schmitz thought: Perhaps it was even stupid of me to offer straight away to be his travelling companion. Yes, it was stupid. Oh, how stupid I am! And why am I stupid? Because I'm a weak character ...

While it is interesting to see how Horváth handles the connecting passages in conversations, this latter-day picaresque novel lacks the dramatic tension of the plays while showing none of the narrative skill that is displayed in his two final novels.

Jugend ohne Gott

The first person narrator

Horváth's previous prose works had used the all-seeing eye of the omniscient author-narrator, and this in part accounts for their indifferent quality: Horváth was first and foremost a dramatist, skilled at creating characters, dialogue and actions. It is therefore understandable that for the two novels *Jugend ohne Gott* (*Youth without God*) and *Ein Kind unserer Zeit* (*A Child of our Time*)—and incidentally for the proposed novel *Adieu Europa* (*Farewell to Europe*)—he chose first person narrators: a teacher, a soldier and a writer respectively. Each one of these three is a character created by Horváth and it is through their eyes that events are seen and narrated. In this way Horváth (not unlike Gide in his *récits*, notably *L'Immoraliste* and *La Symphonie Pastorale*) is able to explore the development of a character without ostensibly making his own comments. Far from being a more personalized style of writing the device of the first person narrator creates a distance between the author and his material; and yet at the same time it encourages a closer identification between reader and narrator, since the reader is invited to share the narrator's innermost thoughts.

On the very first page the reader learns that it is the teacher's birthday (and his age, thirty-four, is significantly close to Horváth's own at the time of writing). While he is not 'zufrieden' (content) he is resigned to his job and its advantages:

> Danke Gott, daß du zum Lehrkörper eines städtischen Gymnasiums gehörst und daß du also ohne große wirtschaftliche Sorgen alt und blöd werden darfst. (*G.W.* 6, p. 281; *J.o.G.*, p. 1.)

> Be grateful to God that you are on the staff of a town grammar school so you can grow old and stupid without any great financial worries.

He is in no way an exemplary teacher and readily admits to his own fallibility, especially where women are concerned:

> Immer muß ich an das Mädel denken, wie es sich reckt und über die Hecke schaut. Ist sie der Räuberhauptmann? Ihre Augen möchte ich sehen. Nein, ich bin kein Heiliger! (*G.W.* 6, p. 310; *J.o.G.*, p. 30)

> I keep thinking of the girl, stretching up to look over the hedge. Is she the robber chief? I'd like to see her eyes. No, I'm no saint!

and a little later:

> Auch ich bin feig. (*G.W.* 6, p. 311; *J.o.G.*, p. 31)

> I too am a coward.

At the school the teacher has already shown his willingness to comply with the political system, even though he balks at doing it. When correcting an essay on 'Why we need colonies' he comes across a particularly glaring example of senseless racial hatred but remembers that it is 'official':

> Ich lasse den Satz also stehen, denn was einer im Radio redet, darf kein Lehrer im Schulheft streichen. (*G.W. 6*, p. 283; *J.o.G.*, p. 3)

> And so I leave the sentence as it stands. A schoolteacher is not entitled to cross out something that has been said on the radio.

From the beginning it is clear that the teacher has a conscience and is aware of compromising his principles, but his own well-being comes first.

Cowardice, self-satisfaction, moral weakness, prurience, all of these are evident in the teacher's behaviour, and yet it is true to say that he is the most intelligent and best educated of Horváth's male characters, and unlike those in the plays he emerges at the end with some sort of integrity. Far from being an objective recorder of events he is a biased critic of them and, as the story progresses, he becomes increasingly entwined in them (here again there is an interesting parallel with Gide's *pasteur* in *La Symphonie Pastorale* whose 'objectivity' collapses as his diary comes closer to the present).

The novel is for the teacher a voyage of discovery: on the one hand he moves from an initially passive acceptance of his role as the instrument of a Fascist state to a rejection of that state and its values; on the other hand he discovers how his individual action can and does influence others, causing them to disentangle the truth from the web of lies woven by them and around them. Eva's admission at the trial that she has told the truth

> Weil der Herr Lehrer auch die Wahrheit gesagt hat (*G.W. 6*, p. 366; *J.o.G.*, p. 86)

Because the teacher told the truth

shows the immediate effect of his behaviour.

Many of the scenes in the novel, and most notably those in the courtroom, require little imagination to transfer them into effective theatrical terms; much of the trial is written in straight dialogue. Because all the events are seen through the teacher's eyes and because he too is 'on trial' there is a tension as powerful as in any of Horváth's plays. By the judicious use of quotation (from Z's diary, newspaper reports, and direct speech reporting) events are seen from different angles: the truth is twisted by everyone, and the teacher's contention that

Die Geschichten sind viereckig geworden (*G.W. 6*, p. 321; *J.o.G.*, p. 41)

Histories have become four-cornered

is rightly in the plural, since historical interpretation applies to everything that happens—interpretation has become not a matter of truth but of choice.

For all his failings the teacher is none the less a character who arouses our sympathies: his job is not a particularly pleasant one and his pupils are for the most part a loathsome bunch. The pangs of conscience that he feels and his reluctance to act can be readily understood, and any reader must hesitate before condemning him outright. When he visits the village priest his thoughts show that he would like to opt out of a dirty adult world and return to the protective shell of childhood and the ideals that he once had:

Und wie ich das Bild so betrachte, bekomme ich Sehnsucht nach meinem Vaterhaus.

Ich möchte wieder klein sein.

Aus dem Fenster schauen, wenn es stürmt.

Wenn die Wolken niedrig hängen, wenn es donnert, wenn es hagelt.

Und es fällt mir meine erste Liebe ein. Ich möcht sie nicht wiedersehen.

Geh heim!

Und es fällt mir die Bank ein, auf der ich saß und überlegte: was willst du werden? Lehrer oder Arzt? Lieber als Arzt wollte ich Lehrer werden. Lieber als Kranke heilen, wollte ich Gesunden etwas mitgeben, einen winzigen Stein für den Bau einer schöneren Zukunft. (*G.W. 6*, p. 313; *J.o.G.*, p. 33)

And as I gaze at the picture I feel a longing for my parents' house.
I'd like to be a child again.
Looking out of the window when there's a storm.
When the clouds are low in the sky, when there's thunder, when it hails.
When it grows dark.
And I remember my first love. I wouldn't want to see her again.
Go home!
And I remember the bench on which I sat and deliberated: what do you want to be? A teacher or a doctor?
Rather than become a doctor I preferred to be a teacher.
Rather than heal the sick I wanted to give something to the healthy, a tiny stone for the building of a better future.

When the teacher does decide to take a moral stand, risking not only obloquy but also the loss of his job, he has developed as a character, he is no longer afraid:

Nein, ich fürchte mich nicht mehr vor Gott. (*G.W. 6*, p. 363; *J.o.G.*, p. 83)

No I am no longer afraid of God.

He is confident and prepared to go through with his duty before accepting the priest's offer of a job in Africa:

Und ich sage dem Pfarrer, ich werde nach Afrika fahren, aber nur dann, wenn ich das Mädchen befreit haben werde. (*G.W. 6*, p. 386; *J.o.G.*, p. 106)

And I tell the priest that I will go to Africa but only when I have freed the girl.

His departure for Africa is for once not a way of avoiding responsibility (as he has done throughout the story), and the last line of the novel shows that the teacher has now become one of those who will no longer connive at Fascism and identifies himself with those who are not tolerated by the Fascist state:

> Der Neger fährt zu den Negern, (*G.W. 6*, p. 406; *J.o.G.*, p. 126)

The nigger is going to the niggers.

The nature of God

In Horváth's earlier works God was frequently associated with money; later he is seen as the cause of disasters, and in the fragment *Charlotte* as the sadistic inventor of all that is evil. In the later plays (especially *Der jüngste Tag*, *Don Juan kommt aus dem Kreig* and *Pompeji*) there is a more obvious concern with the nature of guilt, and in this last play an overtly Christian emphasis. In *Jugend ohne Gott* the title itself (various others e.g. *Die Neger* (*The Niggers*) and *Auf der Suche nach den Idealen der Menschheit* (*In Search of Human Ideals*) had been rejected) announces the theme of the book. Gone is the railing against some malevolent deity, and what remains are perhaps Horváth's most serious comments on the nature of God. It is almost as if there were a resolution of the conflict that had begun while he was still a schoolboy and that had been carried through his entire œuvre.

This treatment of the theme is by far the most serious that the author ever gave it. Even here one must tread carefully, remembering that Horváth himself is at one remove from the teacher. His thoughts on God do not necessarily coincide with those of his narrator, although the similarities in age and experience do suggest more than superficial parallels:

> Es war im Krieg, da habe ich Gott verlassen. Es war zuviel verlangt von einem Kerl in den Flegeljahren, daß er begreift, daß Gott einer Weltkrieg zuläßt. (*G.W. 6*, p. 313; *J.o.G.*, p. 33)

It was in the war that I abandoned God. It was asking too much of an adolescent to understand that God could allow a world war.

This is worth comparing with Horváth's less forthcoming comments on his own adolescence in the radio interview with Cronauer:

> Der Weltkrieg verdunkelt unsere Jugend und wir haben wohl kaum Kindheitserinnerungen. Aber ich denke, wir wollen über diese vergangenen Jahre nicht weiterreden. (*G.W. 1*, p. 9)
>
> The world war casts a shadow over our youth and we scarcely have anything we can call childhood memories. But I don't think we want to go on talking about these years that are past.

On page after page of the novel God is mentioned and the biblical references (in the form of quotations from Genesis and the Gospels) abound. The problem of evil is tackled early on:

> Ja, der Mensch dürfte wohl böse sein, und das steht auch schon in der Bibel. Als es aufhörte zu regnen und die Wasser der Sündflut wieder wichen, sagte Gott: 'Ich will hinfort nicht mehr die Erde strafen um der Menschen willen, denn das Trachten des menschlichen Herzens ist böse von Jugend auf.' (*G.W. 6*, p. 285; *J.o.G.*, p. 5)
>
> Yes, man may well be evil and that is written in the Bible. When the rain ceased and the floodwaters receded, God said: 'I will not again curse the ground any more for man's sake; for the imagination of man's heart is evil from his youth.'

This passage from Genesis (Chapter 8, verse 21) and the following verse (verse 22), had been used before by Horváth in his preface to *Glaube Liebe Hoffnung* (*Faith Charity Hope*), preceded by the telling sentence:

> Und jedem meiner Stücke hätte ich auch folgende Bibel-stelle als Motto voraussetzen können (*G.W. 1*, p. 329)
>
> Every one of my plays could be called *Faith Charity Hope*. And I could have given each one of them the following quotation from the Bible as its motto.

If this passage is taken alone it suggests that evil is so deep-rooted in the human heart that God need only let men have

their free will and evil will prevail. Indeed the passage that is
not quoted* by the teacher bears a remarkable similarity to
the passage from a much older text, that from Anaximander,
read out by the village priest:

> 'Woraus die Dinge entstanden sind, darein müssen sie
> auch wieder vergehen nach dem Schicksal; denn sie müs-
> sen Buße und Strafe zahlen für die Schuld ihres Daseins
> nach der Ordnung der Zeit'. (*G.W. 6*, p. 319; *J.o.G.*, p.
> 39).

> 'To that from which things arise must they return again in
> accordance with their destiny; for they must pay retribution and
> punishment for the debt of their existence in accordance with
> the laws of time.'

There are two statements in the novel that are quite explicit
on the nature of God. The first of these comes from the village
priest:

> Gott ist das Schrecklichste auf der Welt (*G.W. 6,* p.
> 318; *J.o.G.,* p. 38)

> God is the most terrible thing in the world

and occurs in the chapter 'Auf der Suche nach den Idealen der
Menschheit' ('In search of human ideals'). At this point the
teacher is still unable to accept a God who tolerates such evil in
the world:

> Was ist das für ein erbärmlicher Gott, denke ich mir,
> der die armen Kinder straft! (*G.W. 6,* p. 318; *J.o.G.,*
> p. 38)

> What kind of a merciful God is that, I think to myself, who
> punishes the poor children!

The sentence later becomes a leitmotif in his thoughts, and
God appears whenever the truth is revealed. God smiles and

---

* While the earth remaineth, seedtime and harvest, and cold and heat, and
summer and winter, and day and night shall not cease. (Genesis, ch.8, v.22.)
The idea suggested in both Genesis and Anaximander is that just as opposites
exist in nature, creating the cycle of the seasons, so too in human behaviour
good and evil will always co-exist.

withdraws when lies are told. It is not until the penultimate page of the novel that the connection is finally made:

> Denn Gott ist die Wahrheit (*G.W. 6*, p. 405 *J.o.G.*, p. 125)
>
> For God is the Truth

and this second statement, taken with Horváth's own pronouncement on writing 'gegen Lüge und Dummheit' (against lies and stupidity) is the closest that he comes to defining a religious creed. Where so many previous works had used God as a scapegoat or a financial deus ex machina, *Jugend ohne Gott* offers a simple, unambiguous belief in the power of truth.

Style

In Jugend ohne Gott, Ein Kind unserer Zeit and the fragment from *Adieu Europa* there is a visual quality about the text that is striking. Not only are the sentences usually very short but often each individual sentence stands as a paragraph. The language is direct and simple in construction, deceptively so in many instances, since the thought behind it is often far from simple. It is a form of writing that implies urgency and compels the reader's eye downwards rather than along the lines. Frequently, but not always, this is used to build up to a climax:

> Immer stärker wird die Nacht.
> Sie hält mich fest, finster und still.
> Jetzt will ich zurück.
> Vorsichtig taste ich vor—
> Mit der vorgestreckten Hand berühre ich einen Baum.
> Ich weiche ihm aus.
> Ich taste weiter—da, ich zucke entsetzt zurück!
> Was war das?!
> Mein Herz steht still.
> Ich möchte rufen, laut, laut—aber ich beherrsche mich
> Was war das?!
> Nein, das war kein Baum!
> Mit der vorgestreckten Hand faßte ich in ein Gesicht.
> (*G.W. 6*, p. 339; *J.o.G.*, p. 59)

The night grows more and more intense. It holds me firmly,
darkly and silently. Now I want to go back. I grope tentatively in
front of me—With my outstretched hand I touch a tree. I avoid
it. I go on groping—then I recoil in horror! What was that?! My
heart stops beating. I'd like to let out a loud yell—but I control
myself. What was that?! No, that was no tree! With my outstretched hand I felt a human face.

There are often changes in tense from the past into the
historic present, again lending immediacy and building up
tension. The punctuation—combined question-marks and
exclamation marks, double exclamation-marks and
dashes—contributes to the breathless quality of the prose. All
of these factors combined suggest a pattern quite in keeping
with the thought processes of the human mind and this is after
all the author's intention. Frequently he appends such phrases
as 'fällt es mir ein' (it occurs to me) or 'geht es mir durch den
Sinn' (it crosses my mind) which reflect his concern with the
workings of the mind.

Most of the vocabulary used is also marked by its simplicity
and it is only when portraying N's father, the master-baker, or
in the newspaper reports that jargon becomes apparent. The
truth is essentially simple; the lies, hypocrisy and deceit
require a more inflated and contorted form of speech:

'Herr Lehrer' begann er [der Bäckermeister], 'mein
Hiersein hat den Grund in einer überaus ernsten
Angelegenheit, die wohl noch schwerwiegende Folgen
haben dürfte. Mein Sohn Otto teilte mir gestern nachmit-
tag in heller Empörung mit, daß Sie, Herr Lehrer, eine
schier unerhörte Bemerkung fallen gelassen hätten—'
(*G.W. 6*, p. 287; *J.o.G.*, p. 7)

'Sir,' he [the master baker] began, 'my presence here is moti-
vated by an exceedingly serious occurrence which may well have
grave consequences. My son Otto informed me yesterday afternoon in a state of extreme indignation, that you, his teacher, Sir,
had passed an utterly outrageous comment—'

The language of the newspaper report in its interview with
the teacher is even more revealing, both in style and in its

complete contradiction to his real thoughts (a contradiction that he has allowed to pass):

> Der Z sei immer ein aufgeweckter Schüler gewesen, und ihm, dem Lehrer, wären niemals irgendwelche charakterliche Anomalitäten, geschweige denn Defekte oder verbrecherische Instinkte aufgefallen. Unser Mitarbeiter legte dem Lehrer die folgenschwere Frage vor, ob diese Untat ihre Wurzel in einer gewissen Verrohung der Jugend hätte, was jedoch der Lehrer strikt bestritt. Die heutige Jugend, meinte er, sei keineswegs verroht, sie sei vielmehr, dank der allgemeinen Gesundung, äußerst pflichtbewußt, aufopferungsfreudig und absolut national. Dieser Mord sei ein tiefbedauerlicher Einzelfall, ein Rückfall in schlimmste liberalistische Zeiten. (*G.W. 6*, p. 346; *J.o.G.*, p. 66)

> Z. had always been a bright pupil and he, the teacher, had never been aware of any anomalies in his character, let alone defects or criminal instincts. Our colleague then put a grave question to the teacher: did this crime find its cause in a certain brutalization amongst the young—a suggestion which the teacher hotly contested. The youth of today, he said, bore no traces of brutalization and thanks to the general standard of health had, on the contrary, a strong sense of duty, a readiness for self-sacrifice and an unflinching loyalty to the state. This murder was a deeply regrettable but isolated incident, a case of retrogression to the worst days of liberalism.

It is in such passages and in fleeting references to the radio and press that Horváth conjures up the Fascist state. The incipient Fascism of the characters lies more in their compliance than in their actions.

Apart from Julius Caesar none of the characters has a family name, nor is the country mentioned, nor the régime (rather as Brecht called Hitler 'der Anstreicher', 'the house-painter', here Horváth refers to his dictator as 'der Oberplebejer', 'the superplebeian'). This deliberate avoidance of the specific means that the novel cuts across political barriers and holds true for any totalitarian régime.

The fish

The image of the fish is introduced by the bizarre figure Julius Caesar in the chapter 'Das Zeitalter der Fische':

> 'Es kommen kalte Zeiten, das Zeitalter der Fische ...
> ... ich bin zwar nur Amateurastrolog, aber die Erde dreht sich in das Zeichen der Fische hinein. Da wird die Seele des Menschen unbeweglich wie das Antlitz eines Fisches'—(*G.W. 6*, p. 298; *J.o.G.*, p. 18)

> 'Cold times are coming, the age of the fish ... I am only an amateur at astrology, it's true, but the earth is moving into the sign of the fish. There man's soul becomes motionless like the face of a fish.'

As with so many other ideas the fish then becomes a leitmotif in the novel and, by a brilliant use of the image of the net Horváth is able to show both the true murderer T and the teacher implicated. Both are voyeurs, neither reacts spontaneously, and the two are almost fused into one person in the chapters on bait and nets which lead up to the dénouement:

> Es regnet, und das Wasser wird immer mehr.
> Mich schaudert.
> Einen winzigen Augenblick lang sah ich das Netz. (*G.W. 6*, p. 394; *J.o.G.*, p. 114)

> It's raining and there is more and more water.
> I shiver. For one tiny moment I saw the net.

By associating the two characters with the image of the fish Horváth succeeds in creating the impression that the teacher has committed a spiritual murder—he has destroyed in himself all those qualities that T embodied:

> Er kannte keine Schauer, denn seine Angst war nur Feigheit. Und seine Liebe zur Wirklichkeit war nur der Haß auf die Wahrheit.
> Und während ich so rede, fühle ich mich plötzlich wunderbar leicht, weil es keinen T mehr gibt.
> Einen weniger!
> Freue ich mich denn?
> Ja!

Ja, ich freue mich.
Denn trotz aller eigenen Schuld an dem Bösen ist es
herrlich und wunderschön, wenn ein Böser vernichtet
wird. (*G.W. 6*, p. 404; *J.o.G.*, p. 124)

He had no sense of terror, for his fear was only cowardice. And
his love for reality was only a hatred for the truth. And as I
speak, I suddenly feel a wonderful sense of relief because T no
longer exists. One less! Am I glad? Yes, yes I am glad! For in
spite of one's own guilty involvement with evil, it is splendid and
beautiful when an evil-doer is destroyed.

Ein Kind unserer Zeit

The narrator and main character of this last work that Horváth
completed (in the autumn of 1937) is a soldier. As with *Jugend
ohne Gott* the location and date are unspecified, but war is
even more imminent than it had been in the previous novel.
Indeed it reflects Hitler's occupation of the Rhineland (March
1936) and even anticipates the annexation of Austria (March
1938)—the military operation in question is described not as a
war but euphemistically:

Und wir führen keine Kriege mehr, wir säubern ja nur.
(*G.W. 6*, p. 432)

And we don't wage war any more, we are merely cleaning up.

The soldier (like the teacher he has no name) has lived
through unemployment and aimlessness, resorting to petty
theft to eke out an existence, but at the opening of the novel he
proudly proclaims his new-found direction in life: he now has a
place in society, he belongs to the army and feels himself to be
a part of the state. Like so many of the rootless characters in
Horváth's plays (most notably Sladek) the soldier's reasons
for being attracted by the lure of Fascism are only too obvious:

Ordnung muß sein!
Wir lieben die Disziplin.
Sie ist für uns ein Paradies nach all der Unsicherheit
unserer arbeitslosen Jugend—(*G.W.*, p. 412)

> There must be order!
> We love discipline.
> It is a paradise for us after all the uncertainty of unemploy-
> ment during our youth—

It is precisely this sense of gratitude on which Hitler was able to play, using it to build up an army that would be ready at very short notice to help restore Germany's 'honour' and its 'rightful' place as the most powerful military force in Europe.

In this novel Horváth goes even further than he had done in *Jugend ohne Gott* in illustrating the lies and self-deception behind the fine façade. The soldier latches on to his captain, apparently a paragon of state virtues, and follows him blindly. The opening chapters demonstrate this unquestioning loyalty to a leader admirably and, far from alienating the reader, rather make him sympathetic to, or at least easily able to comprehend, the soldier's attitude. Like Sladek he is more victim than villain, and this is characteristic of so many of Horváth's creations. Victims of their own blindness and stupidity they may well be, but in a far more insidious way victims of a propaganda machine that they do not initially understand.

The turning point of the story comes when the captain dies from the bullets of enemy snipers. The soldier risks his own life in an attempt to save him, only to be wounded and rendered unfit for further military service himself. In the dead man's hand the soldier finds a letter addressed to the captain's wife. It is this letter which he eventually delivers, after recuperating from his own wound, and that causes the change in him. Its contents reveal that the captain's death was in fact a suicide: he had gone voluntarily to his death, preferring it to living with the lies about patriotism and honour which he had been incul-cating into his soldiers:

> Verzeihe mir ... aber ich pass nicht mehr in die Zeit ... Es ist eine Schande und was mich am tiefsten schmerzt, ist der Untergang meines Vaterlandes. Denn erst jetzt hat mein Vaterland seine Ehre verloren, und zwar für immer.

Gebe Gott mir die Kraft, daß ich ein Ende machen kann,
denn ich will nicht als Verbrecher weiterleben, mich ekelt
vor meinem Vaterlande. (*G.W. 6*, p. 452)

Forgive me ... but I no longer fit into the times in which we live
... It is a disgrace, and what hurts me most is the downfall of my
fatherland. For it is only now that my fatherland has lost its
honour, and it has lost it for ever. May God grant me the
strength to put an end to my life, since I don't want to go on
living as a criminal; I loathe my fatherland.

Once he has performed this duty, and spent the night with
the captain's widow, the soldier sets off on a search that is
strongly reminiscent of Don Juan's. The girl he is seeking had
been a ticket-seller at a fairground and had once smiled at him;
subsequently she had become an obsession in his mind and
now he goes back to the fairground in the hope of finding her
again. At first no one will give him any precise information, he
is just told that she has 'gone away'; after persisting with his
questions he discovers the truth. She had been made pregnant
by a soldier (and *he* becomes the prime suspect) and had been
sacked fom her job in order that the bureaucratic machinery of
the circus might continue to run smoothly. Then she tried to
get an abortion, was found out and condemned to two years'
imprisonment. In his rage against this injustice the soldier
pursues and murders the circus book-keeper responsible for
her dismissal. As a member of the army the soldier had once
said:

daß der einzelne nichts zählt. (*G.W. 6*, p. 419)

that the individual doesn't count.

Now he hears the circus book-keeper uttering the same sentiments:

... auf den einzelnen kommt es nicht an ... (*G.W. 6*, p.
509)

... the individual is not what matters.

Just as the teacher in *Jugend ohne Gott* had seen an evil
aspect of himself 'die' when T had committed suicide, so here

the murder may be considered as the soldier's destruction of his former self. After committing this symbolic act the soldier's thoughts once again turn to God and Justice, but for him there is no priest to offer him a new job, there is a far bleaker prospect ahead. Like Don Juan he goes and sits in the snow to await death and on the last page he is already frozen and has become a Schneemann.

Here Horváth transcends reality altogether as the dead soldier continues his narration, ending with an appeal to future generations:

> Es sitzt ein Schneemann auf der Bank, er ist ein Soldat.
> Und du, du wirst größer werden und wirst den Soldaten vergessen.
> Oder?
> Vergiß ihn nicht, vergiß ihn nicht!
> Denn er gab seinen Arm für einen Dreck.
> Und wenn du ganz groß sein wirst, dann wirds vielleicht andere Tage geben, und deine Kinder werden dir sagen: dieser Soldat war ja ein gemeiner Mörder—dann schimpf nicht auf mich.
> Bedenk es doch: er wußte sich nicht anders zu helfen, er war eben ein Kind seiner Zeit. (*G.W. 6,* pp. 514/5)

There's a snowman sitting on the bench, he is a soldier.
And you'll grow up and won't forget the snowman.
Or will you?
Don't forget him, don't forget him!
He gave his arm for scum.
And when you are quite grown up, then perhaps times will have changed, and your children will say to you: this soldier was just a common murderer—but then don't abuse me. Just consider: he didn't know what else to do, he was merely a child of his time.

Conclusion

While Odön von Horváth's reputation is well established in Germany, he remains largely unknown in Britain. Since it took virtually twenty years for him to make his mark in post-war Germany, perhaps it is not surprising that he has taken so long to reach this country. Whatever the reasons, there is no doubt that Christopher Hampton's faithful and sensitive translations of his plays will not take long to give Horváth his rightful place in the English theatrical repertoire. Those who suggest that Horváth's language and settings are too far removed from an English audience (and are therefore untranslatable) should take a closer look at the German texts and compare them with Hampton's versions. 'Bildungsjargon' is not just a German phenomenon; nor are the themes of Horváth's work limited in time and place. This is their strength.

Horváth's skill in portraying the mentality that led to the rise of Fascism is seen even in the earliest plays. Even greater is the skill with which he shows that this mentality is not confined to Germany in the twenties and thirties; his themes are as pertinent for this country today as they were for his country of adoption over forty years ago. Whether he is dealing with unemployment, inflation, exploitation, the role of woman, or the problems of individual responsibility, Horváth writes with clarity and instinctive accuracy.

In post-war Germany he has many disciples among the younger generation of writers, and Peter Handke's brief and whimsical essay *Horváth ist besser als Brecht* (*Horváth is better than Brecht*) indicates in its title a sentiment that is not confined to Handke alone:

> Die verwirrten Sätze seiner Personen erschrecken mich, die Modelle der Bösartigkeit, der Hilflosigkeit, der Verwirrung in einer bestimmten Gesellschaft werden bei Horváth viel deutlicher. Und ich mag diese irren Sätze bei ihm, die die Sprünge und Widersprüche des Bewußtseins zeigen, wie man das sonst nur bei Tschechow oder Shakespeare findet. (*Materialien zu Ödön von Horváth*, p. 180)

> The confused phrases of his characters frighten me—the prototypes of malice, of helplessness, of confusion in a particular kind of society are shown up much more clearly in his work. And I like those insane phrases, which show the leaps and contradictions in man's consciousness and which are otherwise only to be found in the works of Chekhov and Shakespeare.

The characters and their language

Horváth's characters are drawn almost exclusively from the 'Kleinbürgertum'. It may seem strange that he, a member of the lower aristocracy and a non-German at that, should have chosen such a social milieu; and yet, as an outsider, he was all the more sensitive in his observation of the 'große Masse' (broad masses) and their language. Perhaps more than any other pre-war writer in Germany he was able to capture the essence of those people who formed the majority of the German population.

It is not that his range of characters is wide; it is in fact quite limited, but it is their representative qualities that are so striking. Whether they be unemployed workers (Schulz, Sladek, Kasimir) or women unable to support themselves (Marianne, Elisabeth) they are almost invariably open to exploitation by their fellow-men. They are victims of inflation and social conditions and yet they are not, as some critics have suggested, stereotypes. Nor are they merely helpless, oppressed victims: some are resourceful and cunning (Figaro,

Havlicek), others are resourceful in their malice (Strasser, Schürzinger) while the main heroes and heroines (Kasimir, Karoline, Marianne, Elisabeth) all display qualities that prevent us from just pitying them.

It is evident again and again from the 'Bildungsjargon' which they talk that they are all alienated, both from one another and from their true selves. The moments when the mask falls are rare ones; most of the time they have no true identity and are readily manipulated by others, whether for personal or political ends. In so-called love relationships money is almost always at stake: Ada pays for Strasser's meagre affections, Valerie's power over Alfred is maintained by her subsidies for his gambling and Alfred even says

> eine rein menschliche Beziehung wird erst dann echt, wenn man was voneinander hat (Act I, scene 1, *G.W. 1*, p. 163)

> any personal relationship, the only thing makes it work is when there's something in it for both of you.

Alongside these characters are the countless petty officials who keep the bureaucracy running coldly and smoothly: policeman, judges, councillors, frontier guards, and even those who work in an Anatomical Institute.

It is hardly surprising that money has become a 'lieber Gott', that human beings are bought and sold (which is quite literally the case in *Pompeji*). So often Horváth's characters are emotionally bankrupt and for them the language of money is the most eloquent one they know. Suddenly all the men want to talk to Christine when they discover that she is rich; Rauch is able to talk to Karoline because he has wealth and position; Alfred and his grandmother can talk, but only in terms of hard cash. Conversations are made up of hollow words and acquired jargon and many a character might utter Karoline's words

> Ich denke ja garnichts, ich sage es nur (scene 52, *G.W. 1*, p. 286)

I'm not thinking anything at all, I'm just saying it.

In all but a few instances these people are incapable of becoming aware of their blindness and stupidity; they will carry on in the same familiar way, like the characters at the end of *Geschichten aus dem Wiener Wald*. It is not hard to understand Horváth's predilection for the circular structure that marks so many of his works.

Horváth's humanity

It would be easy to label Horváth as a pessimist: a writer who saw no light in the darkness and whose vivid and accurate descriptions of sordid slices of life offer little or no humanity, or at best a black humour. His work is pessimistic, and justifiably so, but his compassion is always present. His own creed is a simple one. It is exemplified in his constant battling against lies and stupidity, his striving after truth, and his desire to show

> den gigantischen Kampf zwischen Individuum und Gesellschaft, dieses ewige Schlachten, bei dem es zu keinem Frieden kommen soll—höchstens, daß mal ein Individuum für einige Momente die Illusion des Waffenstillstandes genießt. (*G.W. 1*, p. 328)

> the gigantic struggle between the individual and society, this eternal slaughter-house, where there is to be no peace—but at most the individual may for a few moments enjoy the illusion of a truce.

Horváth was far too modest to suggest that his writing might contribute to the cause of human understanding and compassion. When he died, aged 36, a fragment of the novel *Adieu Europa* was found in his pocket. These are the final lines:

> Warum mußt ich eigentlich weg von zuhaus?
> Wofür bin ich denn eingetreten? Ich hab nie politisiert. Ich trat ein für das Recht der Kreatur. Aber villeicht wars meine Sünde, daß ich keinen Ausweg fand?
> Ich schreibe mein Feuilleton und weiß es nicht. Ich weiß es noch nicht. Das Meer rauscht. Es kommen neue

und neue Wellen. Immer wieder, immer wieder. (*Die stille Revolution*, p. 89)

Why was it that I had to leave my home?

What did I stand up for? I never took part in politics. I stood up for the rights of the human being. But perhaps my crime was that I found no solution.

I go on writing my feuilleton and I don't know the answer. I don't know it yet.

The sea roars. New waves and still more new waves keep on coming. Again and again and again.

BIBLIOGRAPHY

Primary literature

Ödön von Horváth, *Gesammelte Werke 1–8*, Werkausgabe (Frankfurt am Main, Suhrkamp Verlag, 1972).
Ödön von Horváth, *Jugend ohne Gott* (ed. Ian Huish, London, Harrap, 1974).
Ödön von Horváth, *Die stille Revolution* (Frankfurt am Main, Suhrkamp Verlag, 1975).

Secondary literature

Dolly E. Ballin, *Irony in the Dramatic Work of Ödön von Horváth* (Dissertation, Washington, 1969).
Ulrich Becher, *Stammgast im Liliputanercafe*, (in Horváth *Stücke* Reinbek, 1961).
Wilhelm Emrich, *Die Dummheit oder das Gefühl der Unendlichkeit* (in *Geist und Widergeist*, Frankfurt, 1965).
Martin Esslin (and others) *Symposium on Ödön von Horváth* (London, 1977).
Axel Fritz, *Ödön von Horváth als Kritiker seiner Zeit* (Munich, 1973).
Dieter Hildebrandt, *Horváth* (Rowohltmonographie, Hamburg, 1975).
*Dieter Hildebrandt und Traugott Krischke (editors), *Über Ödön von Horváth* (Frankfurt, 1972).

* Particular attention is drawn to these works which contain some of the most important essays and documents on Horváth.

Walter Huder, 'Inflation als Lebensform', in *Welt und Wort*, 25, 1970.

Kurt Kahl, *Ödön von Horváth* (Friedrichs Dramatiker des Welttheaters, 18, Velber, 1966).

Siegfried Kienzle, *Ödön von Horváth* (Köpfe des XX Jahrhunderts, Berlin, 1977).

Jenö Krammer, *Ödön von Horváth: Leben und Werk aus ungarischer Sicht* (Vienna, 1969).

*Traugott Krischke (editor), *Materialien zu Ödön von Horváth* (Frankfurt, 1970).

*Traugott Krischke, *Materialien zu Ödön von Horváths Geschichten aus dem Wiener Wald* (Frankfurt, 1972).

Traugott Krischke, *Ödon von Horváth: Leben und Werk in Bildern und Dokumenten* (Frankfurt, 1972).

Hajo Kurzenberger, Horváths Volksstücke (Munich, 1974).

Ian Loram, 'Ödön von Horváth. An appraisal' (in *Monatshefte* 59, 1967).

Joan Neikirk, *The role of the woman in the works of Ödön von Horváth* (Dissertation, Wisconsin, 1971).

Herta Pauli, *Der Riss der Zeit geht durch mein Herz. Ein Erlebnisbuch* (Vienna-Hamburg, 1970).

Joseph Strelka, *Brecht, Horváth, Dürrenmatt* (Wege und Abwege des modernen Dramas, Vienna-Hannover-Bern, 1962).

Ulrich Weisstein, 'Ödön von Horváth, a child of our time' (in *Monatshefte*, 52, 1960).

Translations

Ödön von Horváth, *A Child of our Time* (comprising the two novels *Youth without God* and *A Child of our Time*), translated by R. Wills Thomas (London, 1938); *Youth without God* reissued as *The Age of the Fish* (Heinemann, 1978).

Ödön von Horváth, *Tales from the Vienna Woods*, translated by Christopher Hampton (London, 1977).

Ödön von Horváth, *Don Juan comes back from the War*, translated by Christopher Hampton (London, 1978).